TOEFL
Final Test 2

반석

TOEFL 급상승 Final Test 2

저 자 박세연, 크리스틴 한, 빅토리아 신, 최종훈
발행인 고본화
발 행 반석출판사
2015년 6월 20일 초판 1쇄 인쇄
2015년 6월 25일 초판 1쇄 발행
홈페이지 www.bansok.co.kr
이메일 bansok@bansok.co.kr
블로그 blog.naver.com/bansokbooks

157-779 서울시 강서구 양천로 583번지 B동 904호
　　　　(서울시 강서구 염창동 240-21번지 우림블루나인 비즈니스센터 B동 904호)
대표전화 02) 2093-3399 **팩 스** 02) 2093-3393
출 판 부 02) 2093-3395 **영업부** 02) 2093-3396
등록번호 제315-2008-000033호

Copyright ⓒ 박세연, 크리스틴 한, 빅토리아 신, 최종훈

ISBN 978-89-7172-769-0 (13740)

반석 TOEFL Final Test 2

영단기 최정예 강사진의 최단기 토플 실전 마무리 테스트

토플 강의를 오랫동안 함께해 온 영단기 최정예 전문 강사들이 한데 모여 이 교재를 만들었습니다. 각 섹션별 전문가들의 노하우가 담긴 이 교재는 가장 최신의 출제경향에 맞춘 실전문제들과 앞으로 출제 가능성이 높은 문제들을 수록하고 있습니다.

그동안 저희 강사진은 토플 현장 강의 및 동영상강의를 통해 쌓은 많은 경험과 자료를 바탕으로 토플 교재의 새로운 패러다임을 만들기 위해 노력해왔습니다. 또한 토플을 준비하는 학생들의 입장에서 꼭 필요한 내용을 담기 위해 많은 시간을 투자했습니다.

이 교재는 토플 시험을 보기 전에 반드시 알아야 할 핵심적인 전략들을 세웠으며, 본인의 실력을 객관적으로 평가해 볼 수 있도록 꾸몄습니다. 이 교재를 통해 여러분들은 실제 토플 테스트와 같은 경험을 해보고 자신의 장단점을 분석해 볼 수 있을 것입니다. 또한, 단순히 교재만 보는 것이 아니라, 이 교재의 내용을 다루는 동영상강의를 통해서 이해가 잘 안 되는 부분들도 완벽하게 집고 넘어갈 수 있습니다. (eng.dangi.co.kr)

저희 저자진은 앞으로도 많은 투자와 연구를 통해서 더 좋은 토플 교재를 만들도록 하겠습니다. 여러분의 유학 생활과 원대한 꿈을 이루는 데 도움이 되는 강사이자 친절한 도우미가 되도록 하겠습니다.

마지막으로, 이 교재를 출간하는 데 많은 도움을 주신 토플 연구진 및 반석출판사 대표님과 편집부원들에게 감사드립니다.

2015년 5월

Reading_ 박세연
Listening_ 크리스틴 한
Speaking_ 빅토리아 신
Writing_ 최종훈

박세연 Reading　영단기 토플 오프라인 마감률 1위 강사

현) 영어단기학교 강남어학원 토플 리딩 대표강사
전) 파고다어학원 토플 리딩 강사(파고다어학원 Best Teacher상 수상)
　　N파고다 토플 리딩 동영상 강의
- 뉴욕주립대 교육학 석사
- 저서 : iBT TOEFL Actual Test Reading – 파고다북스
　　　　Voca For Toefl Reading – 파고다북스
- 동영상 강의 : 파고다 TOEFL VOCA for TOEFL Reading
　　　　　　　iBT TOEFL Reading 기본서

크리스틴 한 Listening　영단기 토플 인강매출 1위 강사

현) 영어단기학교 강남어학원 토플 리스닝 대표강사
　　영어단기학교 토플 리스닝 동영상강의 대표강사
선) 해커스어학원 리스닝 강사
　　파고다어학원 리스닝 강사
- Baruch College 회계학 석사
- The Pennsylvania State University 호텔경영 학사

빅토리아 신 Speaking　영단기 토플 오프라인 마감률 1위 강사

현) 영어단기학교 강남어학원 토플 스피킹 대표강사
　　영어단기학교 토플 스피킹 동영상강의 대표강사
전) 파고다어학원(강남) 토플 스피킹 강사 만족도 1위
　　N파고다 토플 스피킹 강사
- Case Western Reserve University 학사
- Darlington High School

최종훈 Writing　영단기 토플 오프라인 마감률 1위 강사

현) 영어단기학교 강남어학원 토플 라이팅 대표강사
　　영어단기학교 토플 라이팅 동영상강의 대표강사
전) 파고다어학원 토플강사(파고다어학원 Best Teacher상 수상)
　　National Service Center, Philadelphia, Pa ESL강사
- University of Pennsylvania Tesol 석사

최신의 토플 기출문제를 면밀하게 분석하여 실전문제와 유사한 난이도를 반영했다. 전체 문제에 대한 꼼꼼한 해석과 친절한 해설을 수록했기 때문에 혼자서 토플을 공부하는 수험생들에게 많은 도움이 될 것이다. 가장 최신의 토플 출제경향과 실전 난이도를 맞춘 이 교재는 토플 실전 마무리 테스트용으로 손색이 없다.

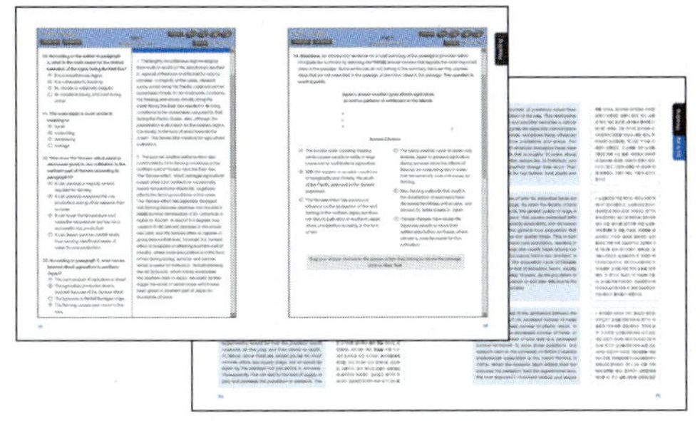

Reading_ 총 3세트 42문제를 제공한다.(1세트당 14문제) 세트당 시험 제한시간은 20분으로 설정하고 문제를 풀어보자.(총 60분)

Listening_ 총 2세트 34문제를 제공한다.(세트당 대화문 1개 + 강의문 2개) 본 교재에서는 각 문제 사이의 간격을 30초로 설정했다.

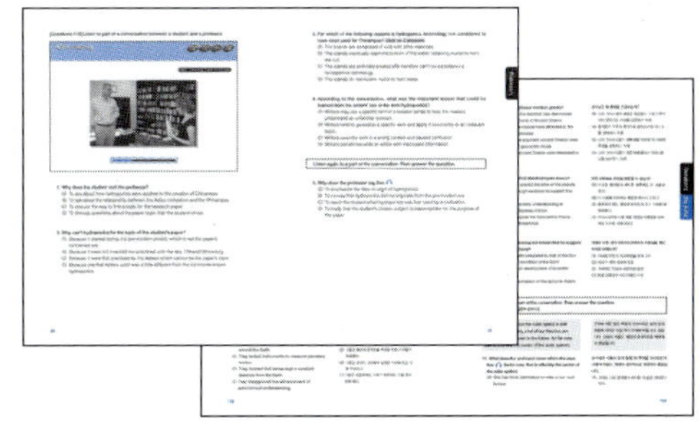

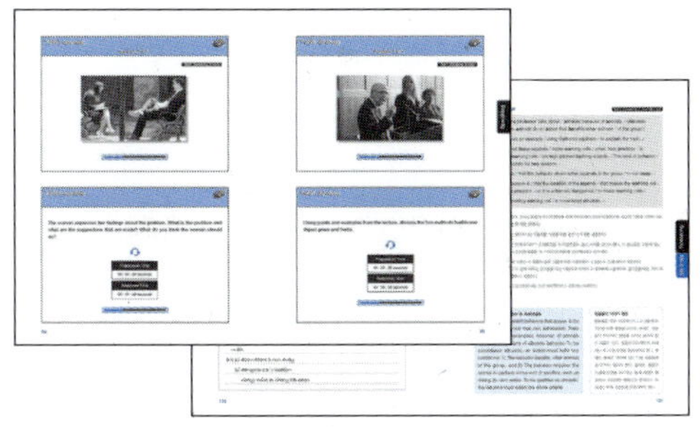

Speaking_ 제공된 음원을 들으면서 녹음기기를 이용하여 제한 시간 내에 답변을 한 후, 샘플 답안을 참고해보자.

Writing_ 각 태스크별로 제한된 시험 시간 안에 라이팅을 작성한 후, 해설의 샘플 답안을 참고하여 라이팅 기본기를 다져보자.

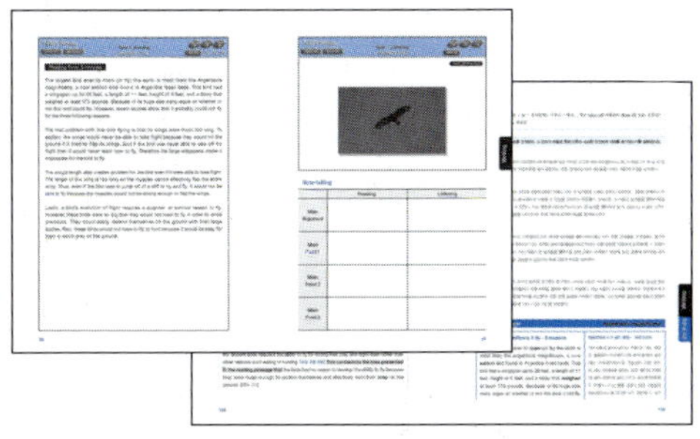

FINAL TEST 02

Reading

Reading Section Directions

This section measures your ability to understand academic passage in English.

The reading section is divided into 2 separately timed parts.

Most questions are worth 1 point but the last question in each set is worth more than 1 point. The directions indicate how many points you may receive.

Some passages include a word of phrases that is <u>underlined</u> in blue. Click on the word of phrases to see a definition or an explanation.

Within each part, you can go to the next question by clicking **Next**. You may skip questions and go back to them later. If you want to return to previous questions, click on **Back**. You can click on **Review** at any time and the review screen will show you which questions you have answered and which you have not answered. From this review screen, you may go directly to any questions you have already seen in the Reading section.

During this test, you may click the **Pause** icon at any time. This will stop test until you decide to continue. You may continue the test in a few minutes or at any time during the period that your test is activated.

You may now begin the Reading section. In this part, you will read 1 passage. You will have 20 minutes to read the passage and answer the questions.

Click on **Continue** to go on.

1. According to the paragraph 1, which of the following is inferred about the flight or flying animals?
   Ⓐ Flight is related to low energy food.
   Ⓑ Flying animal is an ancestor of gliding animal.
   Ⓒ Flying animals have distributed in various places.
   Ⓓ Gliding is less energy efficient way than flying.

2. In paragraph 1, the word extant is closest in meaning to
   Ⓐ available
   Ⓑ remaining
   Ⓒ died
   Ⓓ prevailing

3. In paragraph 1, the word come up with is closest in meaning to
   Ⓐ contribute to
   Ⓑ conceive
   Ⓒ be aware of
   Ⓓ avoid

4. What is the reason for the ability to glide being considered useful to forest-dwelling species in paragraph 1?
   Ⓐ Because gliding serves as a rapid, energy efficient way of descending from trees
   Ⓑ Because gliding provides an advantage of moving through the forest without being exposal to predators in the ground
   Ⓒ Because gliding helps animals to adapt to various forests conditions
   Ⓓ Because gliding enables moving short distances in foraging for food

Gliding Animals

1 A myriad of animals have evolved airborne locomotion, either by powered flight or by gliding. While gliding may be a precursor to some forms of powered flight, gliding has some ecological advantages of its own. Gliding is a very energyefficient way of travelling from tree to tree. Many gliding animals are suggested to eat low energy foods such as leaves and are limited to gliding because of this, whereas flying animals eat more high energy foods such as fruits, nectar, and insects. In contrast to flight, gliding has evolved independently many times among extant vertebrates, and these groups have not distributed nearly as much as have groups of flying animals. Gliding, in particular, has evolved among rainforest animals, especially in the rainforests in Asia where the trees are tall and widely spaced. Some animals use gliding as a technique for fleeing from their predators. It allows them to relocate to other trees without touching the ground. It is also known to be efficient in saving their energy when they forage long-distance prey. Gliding animals have been a riveting area of study for scientists. In recent times, scientists discovered that there is a particular prosperity and diversity of gliding animals in Southeast Asia. This recent discovery led the scientists to come up with some questions: what is the cause of the biological heterogeneity of the gliding animals discovered in Southeast Asia; how could one analyze the reason for the lack of gliding animals in other regions?; And what makes rain forests in Southeast Asia exceptional?

5. The author includes the last sentence in paragraph 1 in order to

Ⓐ provide examples showing that there were many different types of animals

Ⓑ describe events leading up to the events in the following paragraphs

Ⓒ announce the organization of the passage

Ⓓ present a concluding idea to summarize paragraph 1

Gliding Animals

1 A myriad of animals have evolved airborne locomotion, either by powered flight or by gliding. While gliding may be a precursor to some forms of powered flight, gliding has some ecological advantages of its own. Gliding is a very energyefficient way of travelling from tree to tree. Many gliding animals are suggested to eat low energy foods such as leaves and are limited to gliding because of this, whereas flying animals eat more high energy foods such as fruits, nectar, and insects. In contrast to flight, gliding has evolved independently many times among extant vertebrates, and these groups have not distributed nearly as much as have groups of flying animals. Gliding, in particular, has evolved among rainforest animals, especially in the rainforests in Asia where the trees are tall and widely spaced. Some animals use gliding as a technique for fleeing from their predators. It allows them to relocate to other trees without touching the ground. It is also known to be efficient in saving their energy when they forage long-distance prey. Gliding animals have been a riveting area of study for scientists. In recent times, scientists discovered that there is a particular prosperity and diversity of gliding animals in Southeast Asia. This recent discovery led the scientists to come up with some questions: what is the cause of the biological heterogeneity of the gliding animals discovered in Southeast Asia; how could one analyze the reason for the lack of gliding animals in other regions?; And what makes rain forests in Southeast Asia exceptional?

Glossary	⊠

Heterogeneity: composition from dissimilar parts

6. Which of the following does NOT support the tall-trees hypothesis in paragraph 2?
   Ⓐ Lengthy trees enable longer glide range.
   Ⓑ Tall trees enable to prepare in a dive.
   Ⓒ There are hostile environments to populate gliding animals.
   Ⓓ There is lower wind speed between tall trees.

7. Which of the following is the defect in the tall-trees hypothesis in paragraph 2?
   Ⓐ Gliding animals are evenly spread throughout the forests of the Southeast Asian region.
   Ⓑ Most gliding animals are incapable of climbing to the tops of trees.
   Ⓒ Many gliding animals cannot start their glides in short trees.
   Ⓓ Many gliding animals are discovered in forests where trees tend to be relatively shorter.

2 To answer the question of biological heterogeneity of these animals in Southeast Asia, scientists came up with a number of theories. The first theory is often termed the tall-trees hypothesis. The theory suggests that because the trees in Southeast Asia are relatively taller than trees in other regions, the tall trees can offer a resource for longer gliding distances in conjunction with an opportunity to prepare in a dive preceding the gliding. The tallness of Southeast Asian forests is due to the abundance of tropical, lengthy hardwood trees. These trees, with the help of lower wind speeds, accommodate a welcoming environment for gliding, leaving a healthy and diverse environment for gliding animals. Although the tall-trees hypothesis might seem totally accurate, it does contain some notable defects. Firstly, even in the forests in Southeast Asia with shorter trees, which are mainly located in the northern area of the rainforest in China, Thailand, and Vietnam, there exists a diverse environment of gliding animals. Secondly, not all gliders use tall trees to initiate their glides. Some gliders do flourish in low forests, and even metropolitan parks. These show how lengthy trees are not at all necessary for gliding animals. Additionally, countless numbers of gliding animals commence their gliding action at the middle of tree trunks, not climbing to the top of the trees to set off.

8. The word speculation is closest in meaning to

  Ⓐ argument

  Ⓑ thought

  Ⓒ question

  Ⓓ examination

9. The word jeopardize is closest in meaning to

  Ⓐ imply

  Ⓑ initiate

  Ⓒ appreciate

  Ⓓ imperil

10. In paragraph 3, the word This refers to

  Ⓐ Imbalance of trees' height

  Ⓑ Speculation

  Ⓒ Tall trees

  Ⓓ Short trees

3 Second speculation is often called the broken-forest hypothesis. Ecologists speculate that the gliding animals in Southeast Asia jeopardize themselves with descending to the ground or glide to maneuver between trees since the tree canopy contains fewer woody vines that connect the tree crowns compared to the forests in America and Africa. Also, this theory assumes that the top layer of the forests in Southeast Asia is more asymmetrical in height because of the coexistence of the tall tropical trees and other lower trees. This is often beneficial and favored by the gliding animals. It should be noted, however, that ecologists specializing in different regions observed that there is a tremendous local variation in tree height, canopy structure, and abundance of vines depending on various factors including site conditions of soil, slope elevation, climate and local disturbances. Indeed, we can find many locations with abundant woody vines and numerous connections between trees in Southeast Asia and similarly many Amazonian forests with few woody vines.

11. Which of the sentences below best expresses the essential information in the highlighted statement in the passage? *Incorrect answer choices change the meaning in important ways or leave out essential information.*

Ⓐ Ecologists thought that in forests with an uneven canopy structure, gliding is difficult and animals moved to other places where the trees are all about the same height.

Ⓑ Ecologists in other regions have found that gliding animals are as flourishing and heterogeneous in some forests of Africa and America as they are in Southeast Asian forests.

Ⓒ Ecologists have thought that gliding animals are not found in areas of Southeast Asia where trees are connected by vines.

Ⓓ Ecologists have thought that with the fewer woody vines connecting the tops of trees, gliding animals in Southeast Asia are in danger or move between trees.

3 Second speculation is often called the broken-forest hypothesis. Ecologists speculate that the gliding animals in Southeast Asia jeopardize themselves with descending to the ground or glide to maneuver between trees since the tree canopy contains fewer woody vines that connect the tree crowns compared to the forests in America and Africa. Also, this theory assumes that the top layer of the forests in Southeast Asia is more asymmetrical in height because of the coexistence of the tall tropical trees and other lower trees. This is often beneficial and favored by the gliding animals. It should be noted, however, that ecologists specializing in different regions observed that there is a tremendous local variation in tree height, canopy structure, and abundance of vines depending on various factors including site conditions of soil, slope elevation, climate and local disturbances. Indeed, we can find many locations with abundant woody vines and numerous connections between trees in Southeast Asia and similarly many Amazonian forests with few woody vines.

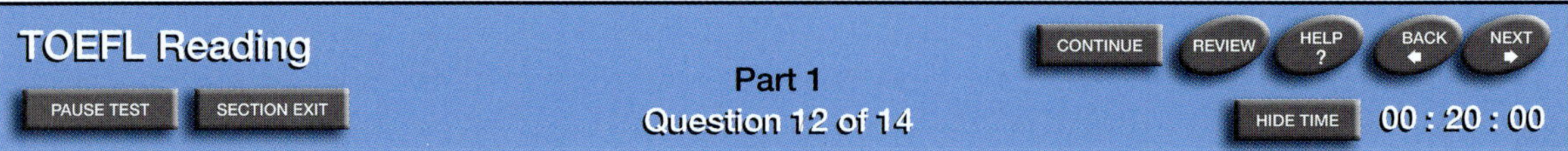

4   The third theory is unique in that it implies that it is the very existence of tall tropical trees themselves that is sponsoring the evolution of gliding animals. This particular theory claims that forests made up of tall tropical trees may be food deserts for animals living in them. Ⓐ ▪ The gliding animals living in tall tropical forests can be classified into two groups: Carnivores that eat small prey such as insects and small vertebrates or leaf eaters. For each group, a tall tropical forest is like a desert in that food resources are few and far apart. For the leaf-eating group, the problem is not the lack of leaves but the lack of edible leaves. Ⓑ ▪ In these forests, tall tropical trees account for approximately 50 percent of more of the total number of canopy trees and over 95 percent of large trees. Ⓒ ▪ However, their leaves contain high concentration of toxic chemicals, being unavailable to be a reliable food source to a majority of vertebrate plant eaters. Ⓓ ▪ The theory suggests that the wide range of travelling across the forest due to the lack of food sources gradually made the animals adopt gliding as a means of navigation since it is more efficient than walking on the ground or jumping between trees. Also, the futility in the number of prey and other insects naturally led various carnivorous animals to forage longer distances for their prey. The irregular flowering and fruiting cycles of tall tropical trees cause this paucity of food, represented by the lack of fruits, seeds, flowers, and seedlings that are the starting point of so many food chains. The lack of prey in tall tropical forests affected geckos and lizards to use gliding, which is the most efficient technique, to move between tree crowns to forage for prey.

12. According to paragraph 4, what problem do leaf-eating animals face in forests with tall tropical trees?

   Ⓐ There is no efficient method of obtaining leaves from trees.
   Ⓑ Trees that have edible leaves are spread out.
   Ⓒ Leaves of most trees are located very high, making animals difficult to reach.
   Ⓓ The tall tropical trees have less leaves than those of other canopy trees.

13. Look at the four squares [▪] that indicate where the following sentence could be added to the passage.

   Due to this, most plant eating gliders avoid eating tall tropical leaves, instead travelling widely across the forest to find edible leaves.

   Where would the sentence best fit?

   Click on a square [▪] to add the sentence to the passage.

14. Directions: An introductory sentence for a brief summary of the passage is provided below. Complete the summary by selecting the **THREE** answer choices that express the most important ideas in the passage. Some sentences do not belong in the summary because they express ideas that are not presented in the passage or are minor ideas in the passage. **This question is worth 2 points.**

Various theories have been suggested to explain the unique abundance and diversity of gliding animals in the rain forests of Southeast Asia.

-
-
-

Answer Choices

Ⓐ The very fact that gliding animals are most ample and flourishing in the forests with short trees represents that gliding did not evolve as an adaptation to an environment of tall trees.

Ⓑ The abundance of gliding animals in different parts of the world corresponds to difference in tree heights.

Ⓒ One view argues that various gliding species have evolved so extensively in Southeast Asia since the forests have been particularly tall; however, the theory remains insufficient.

Ⓓ Jumping from tree to tree or walking in forests that are dominated by tall trees may be less energy consuming compared to gliding.

Ⓔ The tall tropical trees create an environment where most species travel extensively to find food, and gliding may have evolved as a rapid and efficient way of relocating between tree crowns.

Ⓕ The hypothesis that gliding evolved to compensate for a paucity of vines linking tree canopies overlooks the problematic evidence from both Southeast Asian and Amazonian forests.

Drag your answer choices to the spaces where they belong to review the passage, click on **View Text.**

1. The word **fascinating** in the passage is closest in meaning to
   - Ⓐ consistent
   - Ⓑ interesting
   - Ⓒ equivalent
   - Ⓓ fictional

2. The word **this** in the passage refers to
   - Ⓐ timber or ore
   - Ⓑ lack of natural resources
   - Ⓒ settlement in Tigris and Euphrates rivers
   - Ⓓ unstable precipitation

3. Why does the author mention **fascinating** in the passage?
   - Ⓐ To show that the land was qualified to populate
   - Ⓑ To exaggerate that the area was populated by a limited number of people
   - Ⓒ To show that the land was an ideal condition
   - Ⓓ To demonstrate that the area was not the suitable area to live in but people settled in the area

4. According to paragraph 1, which of the following was NOT difficulty that the lands along the Tigris and Euphrates River had?
   - Ⓐ The deficiency of natural resources
   - Ⓑ Low amounts of precipitation
   - Ⓒ Droughts caused by limited amount of snow
   - Ⓓ Thawing snow causing annual flooding

Sumerian civilization

1 Sumer was one of the ancient civilizations and historical regions during the Early Bronze Age. The first civilization could be found along the Tigris and Euphrates rivers in the land, which is now Iraq. It is **fascinating** how these lands were settled by people because there were a variety of challenges that make the area difficult to live in. For example, there were basically little natural resources that the civilization could rely on such as timber or ore. In addition to **this**, rainfall throughout the year was neither constant nor stable due to limited amounts of precipitation and annual floods originated from snow in nearby mountains. Riverbeds were also constantly shifted. Subsequently, this required irrigation system and water channeling to be developed to ensure survival. **As the irrigation system grew to be reliable and the flow of water was controlled, large areas with many people emerged with complex cultures and organization, erecting massive buildings and temples.** As a result, a privileged class emerged to organize these irrigation systems which gained and held power by controlling the dispersal of extra crops.

5. Which of the sentences below best expresses the essential information in the highlighted statement in the passage? *Incorrect answer choices change the meaning in important ways or leave out essential information.*

Ⓐ The increase of capricious giant new cities depended on the ability to control the flow of water via irrigation system in order to build impressive structures.

Ⓑ After the flow of water was controlled, the irrigation system was responsible for the rise of new cities with large population that erected numerous temples and buildings.

Ⓒ As the irrigation system developed and was able to direct the course of water, it became viable for large areas to develop and could develop cultures and organization.

Ⓓ Taking control of the flow of water with developed culture facilitated the growth of impressive temples and buildings.

Sumerian civilization

1 Sumer was one of the ancient civilizations and historical regions during the Early Bronze Age. The first civilization could be found along the Tigris and Euphrates rivers in the land, which is now Iraq. It is fascinating how these lands were settled by people because there were a variety of challenges that make the area difficult to live in. For example, there were basically little natural resources that the civilization could rely on such as timber or ore. In addition to this, rainfall throughout the year was neither constant nor stable due to limited amounts of precipitation and annual floods originated from snow in nearby mountains. Riverbeds were also constantly shifted. Subsequently, this required irrigation system and water channeling to be developed to ensure survival. As the irrigation system grew to be reliable and the flow of water was controlled, large areas with many people emerged with complex cultures and organization, erecting massive buildings and temples. As a result, a privileged class emerged to organize these irrigation systems which gained and held power by controlling the dispersal of extra crops.

6. The word **assumption** in the passage is closest in meaning to
   - Ⓐ composition
   - Ⓑ aggression
   - Ⓒ postulation
   - Ⓓ scrutiny

7. The word **adjacent** in the passage is closest in meaning to
   - Ⓐ neighboring
   - Ⓑ distinctive
   - Ⓒ acute
   - Ⓓ remote

8. In paragraph 2, why does the author mention the city of Eridu?
   - Ⓐ To exemplify the first settlement by farmers
   - Ⓑ To illustrate the simplicity of the culture
   - Ⓒ To compare characteristics of Eridu with those of Uruk
   - Ⓓ To elaborate on the reason why the city was developed

9. According to paragraph 3, which of the following is NOT true about components of early culture?
   - Ⓐ Wandering people
   - Ⓑ Hunting people
   - Ⓒ Peasant farmers
   - Ⓓ Sophisticated building

2 There is an **assumption** that various cities emerged in this area. Examples for such cities can be seen in Eridu and Uruk. The first settlement in southern Mesopotamia was established at Eridu, by farmers who brought with them the Hadji Muhammed culture, which first pioneered irrigation agriculture. This culture was derived from the Samarran culture of northern Mesopotamia. Eridu remained an important religious center when it was gradually surpassed in size by the **adjacent** city of Uruk. The leaders and privileged populations of these cities believed that they somehow had relations to the gods, and believed that they were protected by their own respective patron god or gods.

3 Sumerian had a distinctive style of fine quality painted pottery which spread throughout Mesopotamia and the Persian Gulf. It appears that this early culture was a combination of three distinct cultural influences: peasant farmers, living in wattle and daub or clay brick houses and practicing irrigation agriculture; hunter-fishermen living in woven reed houses and living on floating islands in the marshes (Proto-Sumerians); and Proto-Akkadian nomadic pastoralists, living in black tents.

10. According to paragraph 4, Sumerian writing systems are NOT used for the purpose of
   Ⓐ theology
   Ⓑ management of supply of livestock and products
   Ⓒ engraving letters
   Ⓓ literature

11. According to paragraph 4, what made Sumerian writing system invented?
   Ⓐ A refined administration process
   Ⓑ Process-oriented management
   Ⓒ Increased complexity of organization in cities
   Ⓓ Authority figures

12. According to paragraph 5, which of the following is true about the wheel?
   Ⓐ The origin of the wheel is equivocal.
   Ⓑ A more important impact was gained through the use of the wheel in transportation.
   Ⓒ It is unclear whether the wheel was meant for pottery since it was used for transportation around the same time.
   Ⓓ The use in transportation was not the first purpose.

13. According to paragraph 5, what can be inferred about farming tool before 2900 BCE?
   Ⓐ Bronze tools were not used in farming and war.
   Ⓑ Sumerian didn't use stone and copper tools.
   Ⓒ With an outside culture, the Sumerians learned how to create bronze.
   Ⓓ Before the Sumerians had learned it the skill had been achieved in other societies.

4 In addition, the first form of writing emerged in this area as the civilization became sophisticated, advanced and organized. Deciphered syllabary writing system was developed, which has allowed archaeologists to read contemporary records and inscriptions. Sumerians engraved symbols into damp tablets of clay to write. The name of these symbols that represented words or objects was known as logograms. The Sumerian probably used written characters for the purpose of maintaining inventories of livestock and merchandise as well as literature and theology with most other early alphabets of the time.

5 The wheel that had its origins in pottery was also first invented during this time and shifted to use in transportation. A boxy four edged sled type device on top of four wheels was the earliest depiction of wheel usage. Further technological advances by the Sumerians included the mixing of tin and copper to make bronze, resulting in tools that could be made with sharper edges. Farming tools and weapons were predominately made from bronze after 2900 BCE.

14. Directions: An introductory sentence for a brief summary of the passage is provided below. Complete the summary by selecting the **THREE** answer choices that express the most important ideas in the passage. Some sentences do not belong in the summary because they express ideas that are not presented in the passage or are minor ideas in the passage. **This question is worth 2 points.**

The first permanent groups that settled along the Tigris and Euphrates rivers successfully overcame many challenges.

-
-
-

Answer Choices

Ⓐ The social structure of cities were high divided and held the belief that they were protected through their own respective patron deities.

Ⓑ One particular city of Uruk was unique in that it was protected by two patron gods instead of the typical singular god.

Ⓒ A writing system over time developed that gained efficiency to use a various kinds of areas.

Ⓓ Irrigation system and control of water flow was one of the crucial constituents to develop cities with organization and culture.

Ⓔ Additional breakthrough of this society was the wheel and the invention of bronze, which allowed superior aspects for farming tools and weapons.

Ⓕ Although this society eventually figured out how to make bronze, the skill was not unsurpassed by neighboring cultures.

Drag your answer choices to the spaces where they belong to review the passage, click on **View Text**.

1. The word rather than is closest in meaning to
   Ⓐ despite
   Ⓑ instead of
   Ⓒ in addition to
   Ⓓ related to

2. According to paragraph 1, which of the following is NOT true about portrait?
   Ⓐ It includes drawing, painting, photography, and engraving.
   Ⓑ Its goal is to describe the likeness, personality and the attitude of a person.
   Ⓒ It describes the superficial character.
   Ⓓ The definition of the word is sometimes inadequate to describe portrait.

3. The word stock is closest in meaning to
   Ⓐ apparent
   Ⓑ distinct
   Ⓒ steady
   Ⓓ typical

4. According to paragraph 1, which of the following accurately depicts the development of portrait?
   Ⓐ It became more popular after starting as a secondary art form.
   Ⓑ Due to its static manner, it is a relatively more stable art form.
   Ⓒ It is the very first art form concerned with the personality of the model.
   Ⓓ It has undergone consistent major style shifts.

Portrait

1 Portrait is referred to as a representation or delineation of a person, especially of the face by drawing, painting, photography, and engraving. The purpose of portrait is to display the likeness, personality, and even the mood of the person. Yet, definition like this neglects to capture the sophistication of portrait. Portraits are the products of art that are related to the notions of the character as they are recognized, characterized, and inferred in different eras and regions, rather than to directly try to capture the superficial counterpart. These notions of the character may incorporate gender, age, profession, social hierarchy, and the character of the subject, among other things. Instead of being static, these characteristics are representative of the assumptions and circumstances of the period when the portrait was contrived. It is unattainable to duplicate the notions of characters; it is only possible to evoke or advise them. Therefore, although portraits depict individuals, the artists stress on the conventional or stock types of the subjects rather than their unique qualities. Portrait has also been exposed to constant changes in practice and artistic convention but portraits are still product of prevailing artistic fashions and favored styles, techniques, and media. Consequently, it can be said that portrait encompasses an ample amount of art category that provides a wide range of interactions with psychological, social, and artistic practices and assumptions.

5. According to paragraph 2, what is true of the differences between portrait and other types of art?

Ⓐ Portraits require a collaboration of multiple artists.

Ⓑ Portraits more accurately portray the subject than other forms of art.

Ⓒ Portraits require less time to produce than other art forms.

Ⓓ Portraits require some level of personal interaction between the artist and the subject compared to other art forms.

6. The word Hypothetically is closest in meaning to

Ⓐ Primarily

Ⓑ Particularly

Ⓒ Directly

Ⓓ Theoretically

7. In paragraph 2 why does the author mention an English artist?

Ⓐ To present an example of an artist who adopted a practice in order to reduce the necessary time of sittings of aristocrats

Ⓑ To show used the help of professional drapery artists to help him finish his portraits

Ⓒ To represent it focuses on painting varying body parts of the subject at each sitting

Ⓓ To show it have a wide range of patrons as subjects

2 Considering that portraits are different from other genres or art categories in their crafting method, the content, and the use, they are worthy of being separately studied. ■ First, the production of portraits requires the presence of an individual or their image in most cases. ■ Therefore, the production of portraits accompanies the interaction between the subject and the artist since it requires them to see each other eye to eye. ■ If the subject is of nobility or is busy and unavailable to be in the studio routinely, artists could also use photographs or sketches to finish their portraits. ■ During the 17th and 18th centuries in Europe, sitting times were occasionally reduced due to focusing solely on the head and then employing professional drapery painters to complete the painting. For example, an English artist had with him a series of sketches containing various poses that enable him to solely focus on the head and to lessen the sitting time of the aristocrats. Portrait painter could also be asked to depict the similarities of individuals who were the deceased. For these instances, painters used prints or photographs of the subject to reproduce the image. Hypothetically, portraits could work from the memories or feelings when creating a painting, but this is a rare occurrence according to documented records. Nevertheless, the course of crafting a portrait is intimately associated with the implicit or explicit participation of the model whether it be model sittings, copying a photograph or sketch, or using memory.

8. In paragraph 2, what is NOT mentioned as methods used by painters to create portraits?

Ⓐ Directly observing the subjects during a sitting

Ⓑ Copying a photograph

Ⓒ Using memory to elicit how the subject looked like

Ⓓ Combining traits from a number of subjects

2 Considering that portraits are different from other genres or art categories in their crafting method, the content, and the use, they are worthy of being separately studied. ■ First, the production of portraits requires the presence of an individual or their image in most cases. ■ Therefore, the production of portraits accompanies the interaction between the subject and the artist since it requires them to see each other eye to eye. ■ If the subject is of nobility or is busy and unavailable to be in the studio routinely, artists could also use photographs or sketches to finish their portraits. ■ During the 17th and 18th centuries in Europe, sitting times were occasionally reduced due to focusing solely on the head and then employing professional drapery painters to complete the painting. For example, an English artist had with him a series of sketches containing various poses that enable him to solely focus on the head and to lessen the sitting time of the aristocrats. Portrait painter could also be asked to depict the similarities of individuals who were the deceased. For these instances, painters used prints or photographs of the subject to reproduce the image. Hypothetically, portraits could work from the memories or feelings when creating a painting, but this is a rare occurrence according to documented records. Nevertheless, the course of crafting a portrait is intimately associated with the implicit or explicit participation of the model whether it be model sittings, copying a photograph or sketch, or using memory.

9. According to paragraph 3, portrait is viewed as being of a lower status because of

Ⓐ innovation

Ⓑ copy

Ⓒ perfectionism

Ⓓ creativity

10. The word cursory is closest in meaning to

Ⓐ misunderstanding

Ⓑ famous

Ⓒ superficial

Ⓓ insignificant

11. According to paragraph 3, what can be inferred about Michelangelo's view of portrait?

Ⓐ He believed that imitation was a requirement for creativity.

Ⓑ He felt that portrait art should be examined as a form of fine art.

Ⓒ He believed that portraits should portray idealized beauty.

Ⓓ He thought that subjects should rather be from the ancient times than contemporary.

12. The author in paragraph 3 discusses Picasso as an example of an artist who

Ⓐ modified the way other artists felt about portrait art

Ⓑ relied solely on portrait to rise to fame

Ⓒ had scarcely any theoretical opposition to portrait than most modern artists

Ⓓ drew portraits despite his doubts about portrait being a fine art form

3 Not to mention, portrait can be set apart from other artistic genres such as still life, landscape, and history by its relevance with appearance, or likeness. Consequently, the genre of portrait received its disapproval for copying instead of for artistic originality or inspiration; therefore portrait is sometimes viewed as inferior to other artistic genres. This notion is well shown in the Renaissance art theory, where portrait became associated with the degree of cursory imitation as opposed to fine art, which was linked with originality and inspiration. One of the examples of the prevailing attitude towards portrait is Michelangelo's renowned objection to painting portrait, not having ideally beautiful models to portrait. Satirically, many made their living through portrait. During the 19th and 20th centuries when modernism prevailed, the reception towards portrait was critical. Portrait maintained to survive despite its theoretical criticisms. For example, Picasso became well known for his cubist stilllife drawings in his initial career, but some of the most impressive experiments in this new style were his portraits of art dealers.

2 Considering that portraits are different from other genres or art categories in their crafting method, the content, and the use, they are worthy of being separately studied. Ⓐ ▪ First, the production of portraits requires the presence of an individual or their image in most cases. Ⓑ ▪ Therefore, the production of portraits accompanies the interaction between the subject and the artist since it requires them to see each other eye to eye. Ⓒ ▪ If the subject is of nobility or is busy and unavailable to be in the studio routinely, artists could also use photographs or sketches to finish their portraits. Ⓓ ▪ During the 17th and 18th centuries in Europe, sitting times were occasionally reduced due to focusing solely on the head and then employing professional drapery painters to complete the painting. For example, an English artist had with him a series of sketches containing various poses that enable him to solely focus on the head and to lessen the sitting time of the aristocrats. Portrait painter could also be asked to depict the similarities of individuals who were the deceased. For these instances, painters used prints or photographs of the subject to reproduce the image. **Hypothetically**, portraits could work from the memories or feelings when creating a painting, but this is a rare occurrence according to documented records. Nevertheless, the course of crafting a portrait is intimately associated with the implicit or explicit participation of the model whether it be model sittings, copying a photograph or sketch, or using memory.

13. Look at the four squares [▪] that indicate where the following sentence could be added to the passage.

Occasionally, portrait artists should have direct or indirect relationships with their subjects.

Where would the sentence best fit?

Click on a square [▪] to add the sentence to the passage.

14. Directions: An introductory sentence for a brief summary of the passage is provided below. Complete the summary by selecting the **THREE** answer choices that express the most important ideas in the passage. Some sentences do not belong in the summary because they express ideas that are not presented in the passage or are minor ideas in the passage. **This question is worth 2 points.**

Portrait as an art form is more complex than is suggest by its definition.

-
-
-

Answer Choices

Ⓐ The dictionary has consistently changed the definition of portrait art throughout the years to manifest the shifting attitudes regarding the genre.

Ⓑ Portrait art should be classified as a unique artistic genre due to its relation with the subject and the way in which it was formed.

Ⓒ Portrait art was at times viewed negatively since it was characterized as simple copying, lacking of artistic originality.

Ⓓ Starting in the Renaissance and continuing into the start of the nineteenth century, portrait art was admired to a greater extent than it is today.

Ⓔ Portraits generally represent the conventions of the time rather than the distinct qualities of the individual.

Ⓕ Majority of artists throughout history avoided portrait art since it was regarded as a mechanical art form.

Drag your answer choices to the spaces where they belong to review the passage, click on **View Text**.

Listening

Listening Section Directions

This section measures your ability to understand conversations and lectures in English. The listening section is divided into 2 separately timed parts. In each part you will listen to 1 conversation and 2 lectures. You will hear each conversation or lecture only one time.

After each conversation or lecture, you will answer some questions about it. The questions typically ask about the main idea and supporting details. Some questions ask about a speaker s purpose and attitude. Answer the questions based on what is stated or implied by the speakers.

You may take notes while you listen. You may use your notes to help you answer the questions. Your notes will not be scored.

If you need to change the volume while you listen, click on the Volume icon at the top of the screen.

In some questions, you will see this icon: ∩ This means that you will hear, but not see part of the question. Some of the questions have special directions. These directions appear in a gray box on the screen.

Most questions are worth one point. If a question is worth more than one point, it will have special directions that indicate how many points you can receive.

You must answer each question. After you answer, click on Next. Then click on OK to confirm your answer and go on to the next question. After you click on OK, you cannot return to previous questions.

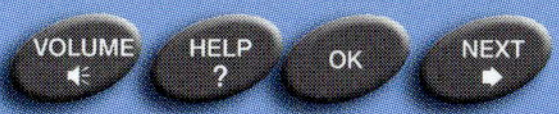

Test2_Listening_Part1_00_Direction.mp3

Listening Directions

In this part, you will listen to 1 conversation and 2 lectures.

You must answer each question. After you answer, click on Next. Then click on OK to confirm your answer and go on to the next question. After you click on OK, you cannot return to previous questions.

You may now begin this part of the Listening Section.

Listening

[Questions 1-5] Listen to part of a conversation between a student and a professor.

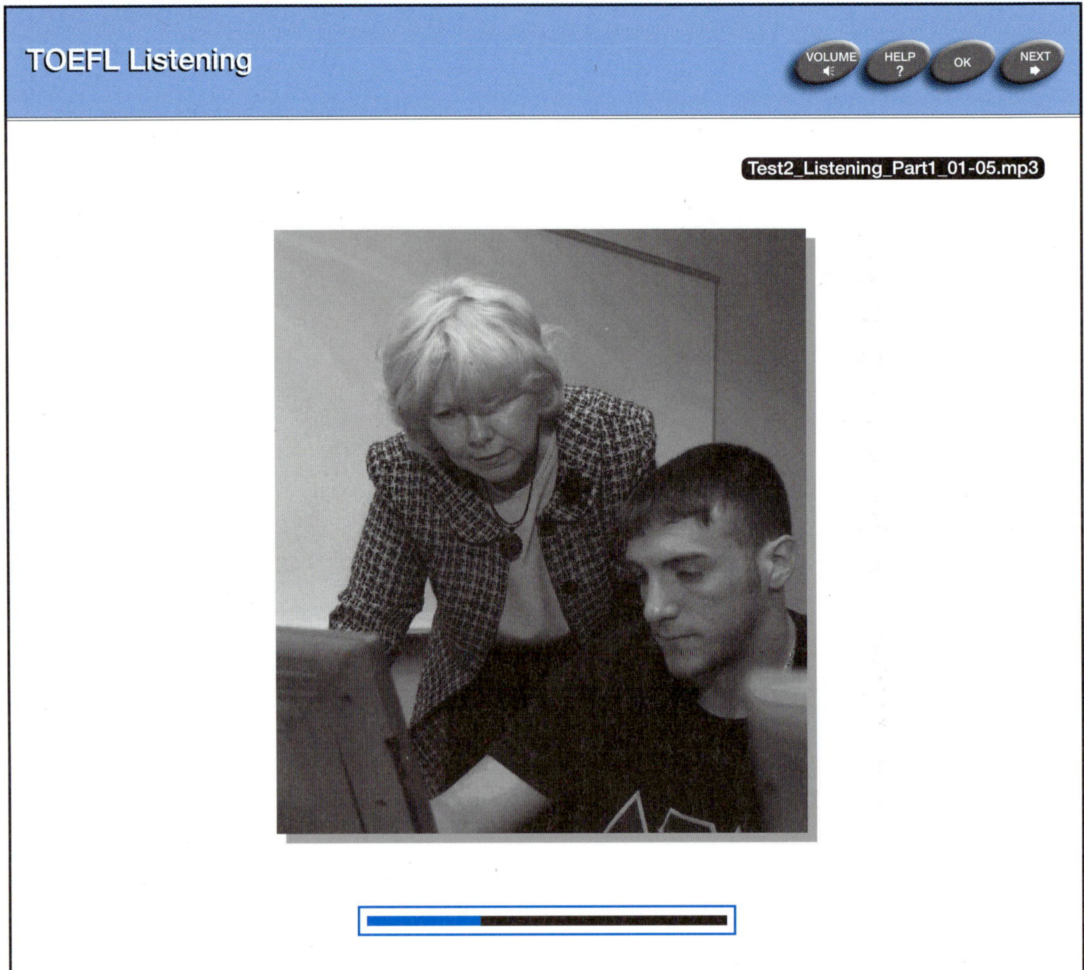

1. **Why does the man go to the professor's office ?**
   Ⓐ To apologize that he was late at the meeting due to a doctor's appointment
   Ⓑ To receive the professor's feedback and reaction on his essay
   Ⓒ To discuss John Dewey's philosophy with the professor
   Ⓓ To ask about the political science meeting on John Dewey

---

Listen again to a part of the conversation. Then answer the question.

---

2. **Why does the professor say this:** 🎧
   Ⓐ To indicate that her own writing needs a lot of editing
   Ⓑ To imply that it's necessary for the student to edit his writing
   Ⓒ To imply that the student's work is not good to submit
   Ⓓ To contrast the student's tendency to edit before writing

3. What are the two technical flaws that the professor point out in the student's essay? Click on 2 answers.
   Ⓐ The essay could be presented in a more logical order.
   Ⓑ The essay contains irrelevant information that could be cut out.
   Ⓒ The essay did not include the biographical information of John Dewey.
   Ⓓ The essay is not organized in chronological order.

4. Why does the professor recommend the student to lead the discussion for the political science club meeting?
   Ⓐ The student needs to help Tom Hayward who does not know anything about John Dewey.
   Ⓑ The student can receive help revising his essay on John Dewey.
   Ⓒ The student might be qualified for discussing the topic.
   Ⓓ The student wants to learn more about John Dewey in order to write a better essay on him.

Listen again to a part of the conversation. Then answer the question.

---

5. What does the student mean when he says:
   Ⓐ The student will attend the meeting if he heals from his injuries.
   Ⓑ The student wants to receive a good score on his papers.
   Ⓒ The student will make sure to attend the meeting.
   Ⓓ The student realizes that attending the meeting will leave a good impression with the professor.

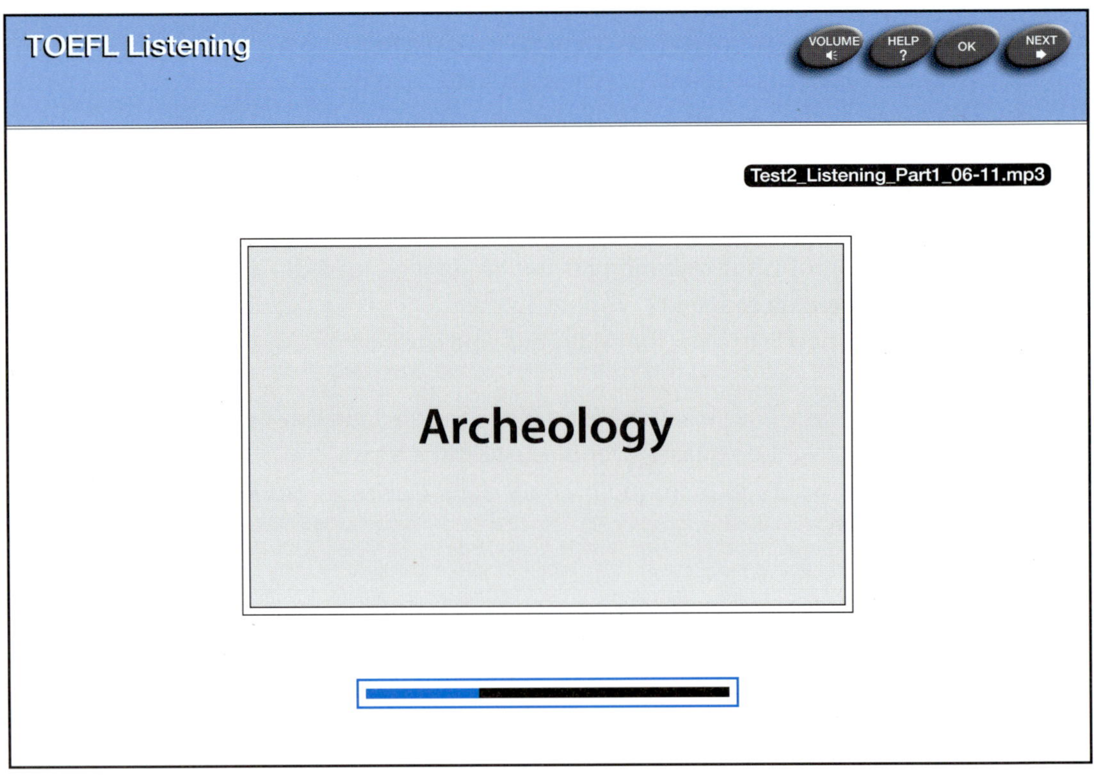
TOEFL Listening
VOLUME
HELP
?
OK
NEXT
Test2_Listening_Part1_06-11.mp3
Archeology

TOEFL Listening
VOLUME
HELP
?
OK
NEXT

6. **What does the professor mainly discuss?**
   - Ⓐ Widely accepted myths concerning the study of archaeology
   - Ⓑ A historical site that was excavated with the aid of a muon detector
   - Ⓒ The combination of physics and archaeology to develop a technology
   - Ⓓ Positive aspects of muon detectors for archaeologists

7. **According to the professor, why are muon used in archaeology?**
   - Ⓐ Because they can carry and transmit electrical charges
   - Ⓑ Because they degrade cosmic rays into more basic components
   - Ⓒ Because they travel through solid material
   - Ⓓ Because they can produce 3-D pictures

8. **What can a muon detector reveal about the Colosseum?**
   - Ⓐ The darkness of the inner region
   - Ⓑ The structure of underground rooms
   - Ⓒ The strength of its foundation
   - Ⓓ The material composing the walls

9. **Why does the professor mention CT scans?**
   - Ⓐ To discuss the possibility of using muon detectors in medicine
   - Ⓑ To compare archaeological diagrams with medical ones
   - Ⓒ To emphasize the role of technology in scientific fields
   - Ⓓ To explain the imaging process of muon detectors

10. **Why were muon detectors unpopular in 1967? Click on 3 answers.**
   - Ⓐ They were expensive to build.
   - Ⓑ They required an energy source.
   - Ⓒ They were too large.
   - Ⓓ They were slow to produce an image.
   - Ⓔ They could not scan in all directions.

11. **What does the professor imply about newer muon detectors?**
   - Ⓐ They can be used to develop clean energy.
   - Ⓑ They will gain popularity among archaeologists.
   - Ⓒ They have potential in several scientific fields.
   - Ⓓ They are more accurate than older detectors.

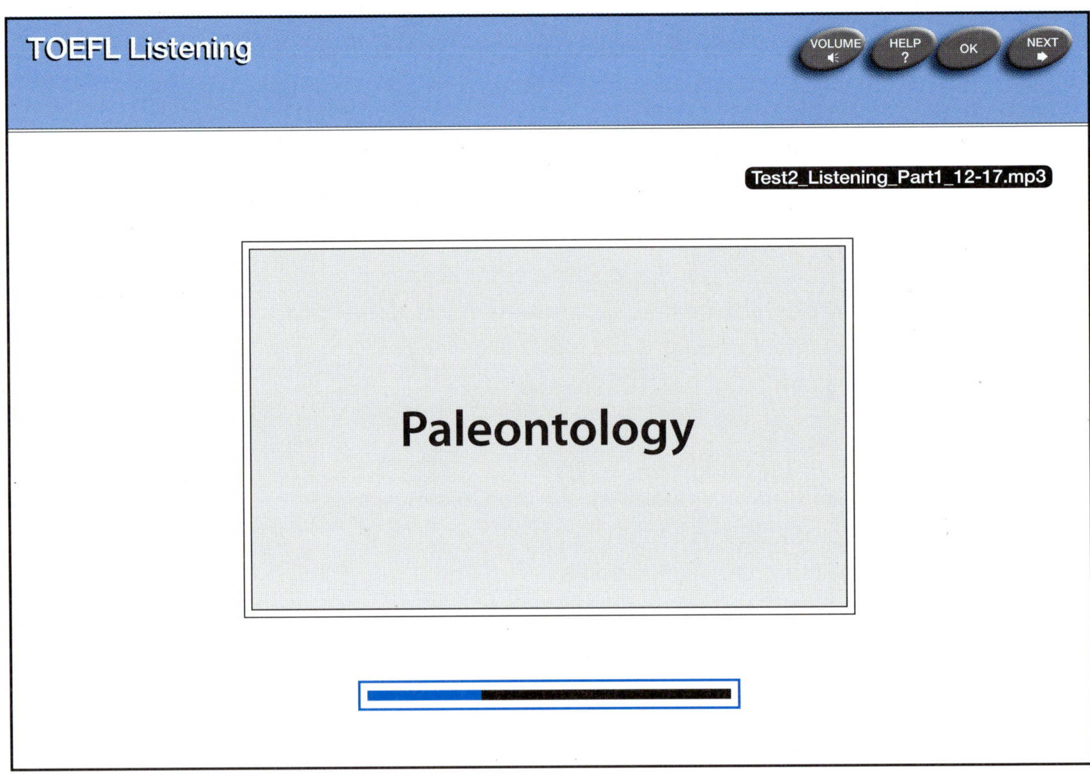

TOEFL Listening
VOLUME
HELP ?
OK
NEXT
Test2_Listening_Part1_12-17.mp3
Paleontology

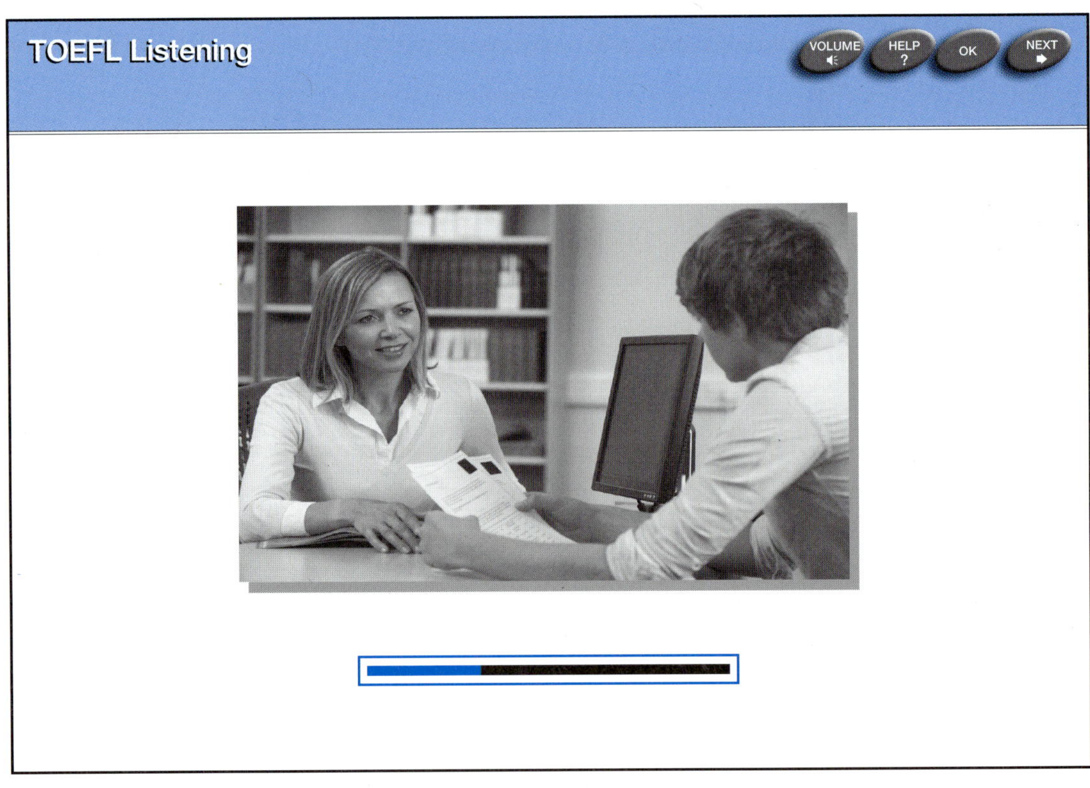

TOEFL Listening
VOLUME
HELP ?
OK
NEXT

12. **What is the lecture mainly about?**
    Ⓐ Describing the digestion mechanics of the sauropods
    Ⓑ Discussing the proposals about the adaptation of recessive animals
    Ⓒ Illustrating the difficulties faced by the sauropods while evolving
    Ⓓ Comparing the differences of sauropods and ocean blue whales

13. **Why does the professor mention the blue whales?**
    Ⓐ To introduce a contemporary counterpart of sauropods that live in the oceans
    Ⓑ To emphasize the size and biological features of sauropods
    Ⓒ To illustrate how big the blue whales are compared to sauropods
    Ⓓ To emphasize the impressive size of blue whales

> Listen again to a part of the conversation. Then answer the question.

14. **Why does the professor say this:** 🎧
    Ⓐ She wants the students to challenge this assertion.
    Ⓑ She thinks this number is very impressive.
    Ⓒ She does not think this information is reliable.
    Ⓓ She thinks this information is particularly important.

15. **Why does the professor mention potatoes?**
    Ⓐ To support that sauropods could not have controlled their temperature internally
    Ⓑ To imply that sauropods struggled to regulate their temperature because the Earth was too hot
    Ⓒ To emphasize that many warm-blooded animals have thrived on the Earth
    Ⓓ To illustrate that sauropods are too big to be compared to potatoes

16. **According to the professor, how did sauropods manage with a shortage of food?**
    Ⓐ Plantations provided a variety of plants as food.
    Ⓑ Slow digestion allowed the efficient use of energy.
    Ⓒ Food that did not require chewing was plentiful.
    Ⓓ Gastroliths supplied necessary minerals.

> Listen again to a part of the conversation. Then answer the question.

17. **What does the professor mean when she says this:** 🎧
    Ⓐ People should learn about sauropods' digestive pattern.
    Ⓑ People should conduct more research on the behavior of sauropods.
    Ⓒ Sauropods' way of adaptation is extremely efficient.
    Ⓓ Sauropods are more intelligent than human beings in some ways.

반석
TOEFL
급상승
Final Test 2

Listening Directions

In this part, you will listen to 1 conversation and 2 lectures.

You must answer each question. After you answer, click on Next. Then click on OK to confirm your answer and go on to the next question. After you click on OK, you cannot return to previous questions.

You may now begin this part of the Listening Section.

[Questions 1-5] Listen to part of a conversation between a student and a professor.

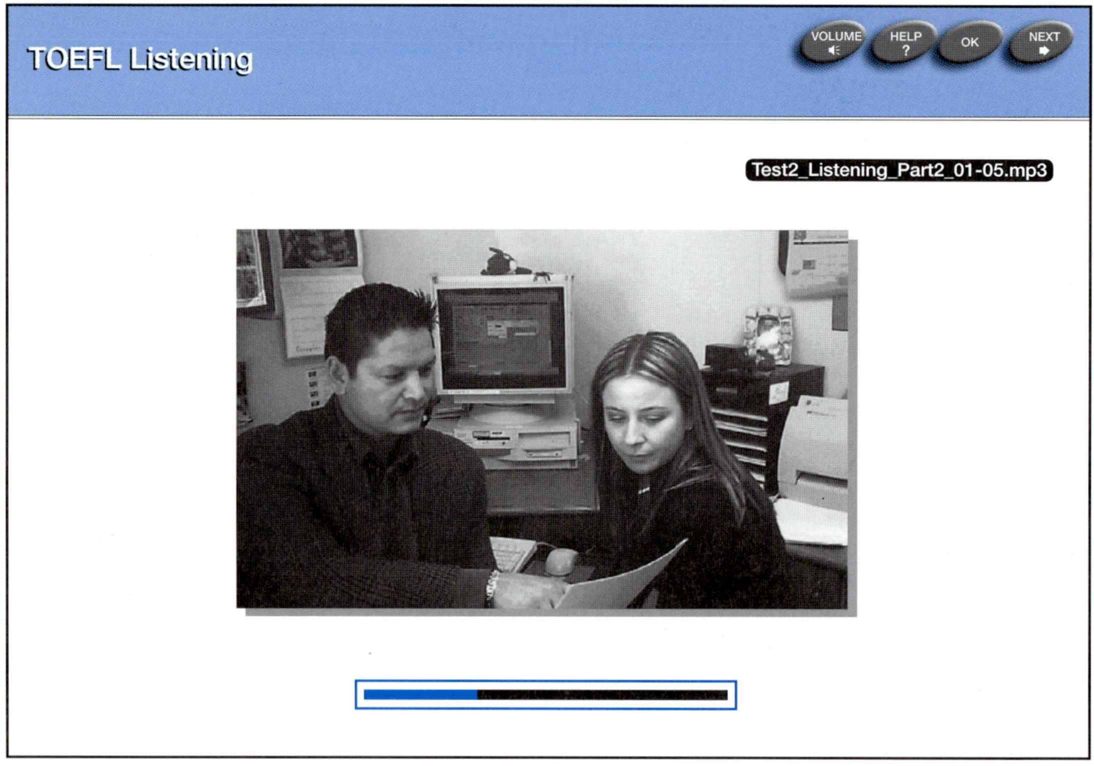

1. What is the conversation about?
   Ⓐ The problems about defining test subjects
   Ⓑ The submission of a proposal by Friday
   Ⓒ The student's problem with analyzing statistics
   Ⓓ The need for improvements in the proposal

2. Why does the professor mention the Computer Center?
   Ⓐ The student should search the Web for statistical information.
   Ⓑ The student could receive specific advice about choosing test subjects.
   Ⓒ The student can find Jess who is a helpful woman at the information desk.
   Ⓓ The student may get some help setting up the statistical analysis.

3. According to the professor, how should the student modify her proposal?
   Ⓐ She should outline the process of choosing her statistical analysis.
   Ⓑ She should define the meaning of her statistics.
   Ⓒ She should explain more about the selection of her subjects.
   Ⓓ She should add personal information about the international students.

Listen again to a part of the conversation. Then answer the question.

4. **Why does the professor say this:**
   Ⓐ To indicate a shortcoming in the student's proposal
   Ⓑ To contrast two different kinds of language speakers
   Ⓒ To illustrate the dissimilar linguistic levels of international students
   Ⓓ To emphasize the variety of subjects for the student's research

5. **What does the professor imply about the people in the committee?**
   Ⓐ They will expect her to go to the Computer Center.
   Ⓑ They probably don't understand the stress patterns she is researching.
   Ⓒ They will question her process of comparing test subjects.
   Ⓓ They will be particularly selective and discriminating toward her.

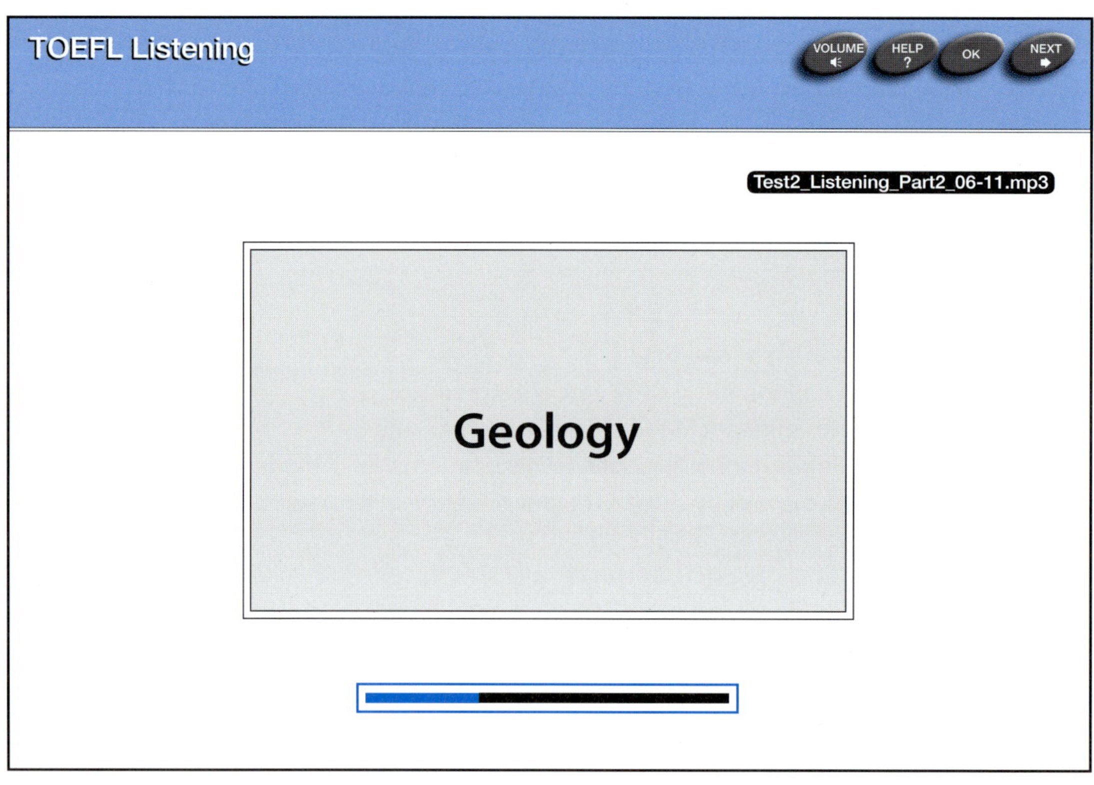

TOEFL Listening
VOLUME
HELP
?
OK
NEXT
Test2_Listening_Part2_06-11.mp3
Geology

TOEFL Listening
VOLUME
HELP
?
OK
NEXT

6. What is the main topic of the lecture?
   Ⓐ Explaining the importance of uniformitarianism
   Ⓑ Describing a theory about a previously inexplicable geological feature
   Ⓒ Illustrating how uniformitarianists' neglected counteracting hypothesis
   Ⓓ Proving the different theories concerning a geological feature

---

Listen again to a part of the conversation. Then answer the question.

---

7. What does the professor mean when he says this: 🎧
   Ⓐ He thinks the students missed a point he made earlier.
   Ⓑ He realizes he forgot to mention something important.
   Ⓒ He does not want the students to miss the key points.
   Ⓓ He wants to return to a concept he referred to previously.

8. Why does the professor mention Charles Darwin?
   Ⓐ To highlight that uniformitarianism was important in various fields.
   Ⓑ To provide an example of a scientist who invented uniformitarianism
   Ⓒ To inform that Charles Darwin applied the concept of uniformitarianism to his
      research
   Ⓓ To illustrate how uniformitarianism affected Charles Darwin

9. Why were the opponents to Bretz's hypothesis unable to discredit it? Click on 2
   answers.
   Ⓐ Bretz's hypothesis contained a lot of uniformitarianism concepts.
   Ⓑ Bretz's hypothesis could only explain certain isolated parts of the scabland.
   Ⓒ Bretz's hypothesis was used against a concept of uniformitarianism.
   Ⓓ A lot of evidence was found in support of Bretz's hypothesis.
   Ⓔ Bretz's hypothesis accounted for the entire formation of scabland geography.

10. According to the professor's explanation at the end of the lecture, which one
    of the following describes the correct characteristic of the theory on how the
    channeled scabland was formed?
    Ⓐ Uniformitarianism is the most accurate explanation for how the channeled
       scabland was gradually formed.
    Ⓑ Bretz's theory is the most accurate explanation for how the channeled scabland
       as it was formed by a single catastrophic event.
    Ⓒ Both uniformitarianism and Bretz's ideas did not correctly represent how the
       scabland was formed.
    Ⓓ Both uniformitarianism and Bretz's ideas were correct, because the channeled
       scabland was formed by a series of catastrophic and gradual events.

11. What does the professor imply when he says this: 🎧

Ⓐ He's angry that many people ignore uniformitarianism.

Ⓑ He thinks that people are responsible for disregarding uniformitarianism.

Ⓒ He believes uniformitarianism is still acceptable to explain geological features.

Ⓓ He wants to express his disdain for uniformitarianism.

[Questions 12-17] Listen to part of a lecture in an astronomy class.

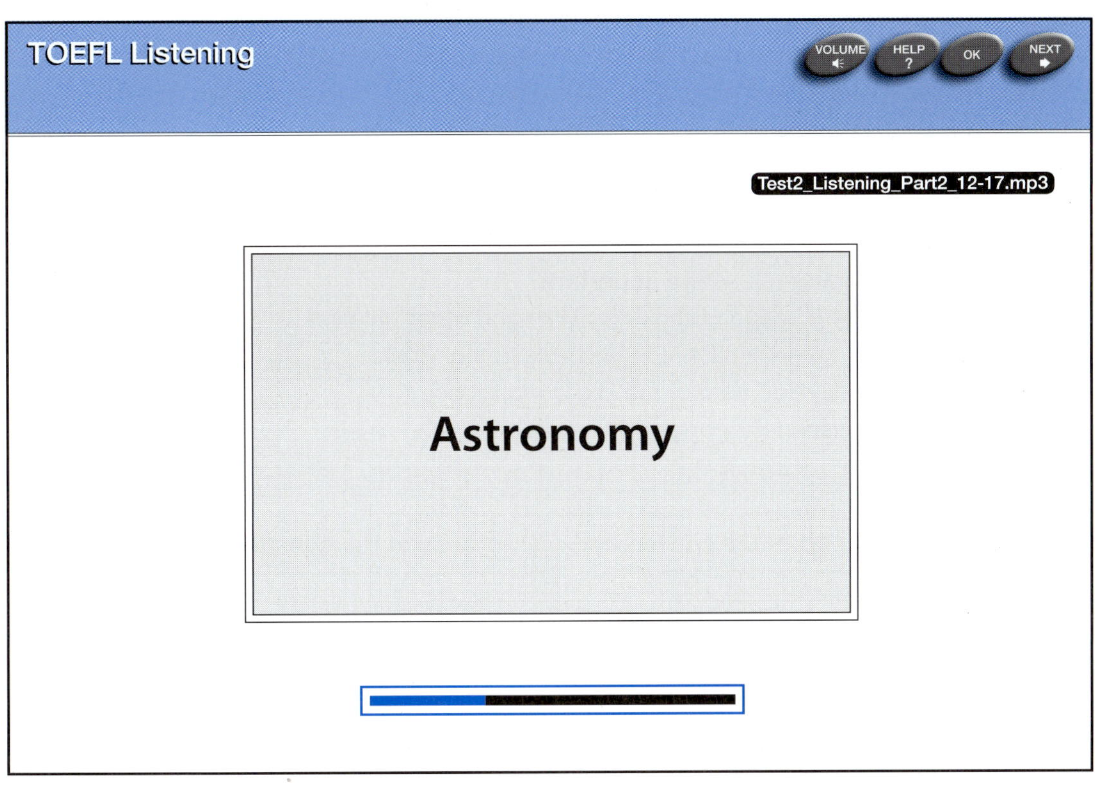

12. **What does the professor primarily discuss?**
    Ⓐ The Big Bang Theory and its scientific importance
    Ⓑ Astronomical techniques in astronomythat shaped our perspective of the
       universe
    Ⓒ The contrast between two competing types of telescopes
    Ⓓ Various rolesof computers in producing high-resolution images

13. **Why is the Hooker telescope important?**
    Ⓐ It showed the creation of the Milky Way and other galaxies.
    Ⓑ It was the most sophisticated telescope in the 1930s.
    Ⓒ It aided the development of the Big Bang theory.
    Ⓓ It utilized several telescopes and computers.

Listen again to a part of the conversation. Then answer the question.

---

14. **What does the professor imply when he says this:** 🎧
    Ⓐ He omitted some of the more difficult and complex ideas.
    Ⓑ The students should review their lecture notes carefully.
    Ⓒ The students should study the concept on their own time.
    Ⓓ He thinks that the students cannot understand the telescope because of its
       complexity.

15. **According to the professor, why is it difficult to create an image with an
    interferometer?**
    Ⓐ Pipes connecting the telescopes with computers are thousands of meters long.
    Ⓑ Telescopes require frequent and expensive maintenance.
    Ⓒ Telescope operators lack sufficient knowledge about imaging computers.
    Ⓓ Multiple images have to be synchronized into one complete image.

16. **Why does the professor mention their observation of Castor?**
    Ⓐ To point out an advantage of advanced technology
    Ⓑ To bring up a problem with conventional telescopes
    Ⓒ To note the presence of multiple stars in some celestial bodies
    Ⓓ To emphasize the importance of the 6 surrounding stars

17. What does the professor imply when he says this: 🎧
- Ⓐ The next lecture will be about the sustenance of life on other planets.
- Ⓑ The professor expects students to understand the meaning of life on Earth.
- Ⓒ The professor thinks the advanced technology could result in scientific progress.
- Ⓓ The professor emphasizes the importance of the particular discovery.

Speaking

`Test2_Speaking_Direction.mp3`

Speaking Section Directions

In this section of the test, you will be able to demonstrate your ability to speak about a variety of topics. You will answer six questions by speaking into the microphone. Answer as thoroughly as possible.

In questions 1 and 2, you will speak about familiar topics. Your response will be scored on your ability to speak clearly and coherently about the topics.

In questions 3 and 4, you will first read a short text. You will then listen to a talk on the same topic. You will need to combine appropriate information from the text and the talk to provide a complete answer to the question. Your response will be scored on your ability to speak clearly and coherently about what you have read and heard.

In questions 5 and 6, you will listen to part of a conversation or a lecture. You will then be asked a question about what you heard. Your response will be scored on your ability to speak clearly and coherently about what you have heard.

You may take notes while you read and while you listen to the conversations and lectures. You may use your notes to help prepare your response.

Listen carefully to the directions for each question. The directions will not be written on the screen.

For each question you will be given a short time to prepare your response. A clock will show how much preparation time is remaining. When the preparation time is up, you will be told to begin your response. A clock will show how much response time is remaining. A message will appear on the screen when the response time has ended.

Test2_Speaking_1.mp3

Among intelligence, creativity and courage, what is the most important quality that a person should have? State your opinion and explain why.

Preparation Time
00 : 00 : 15 seconds

Response Time
00 : 00 : 45 seconds

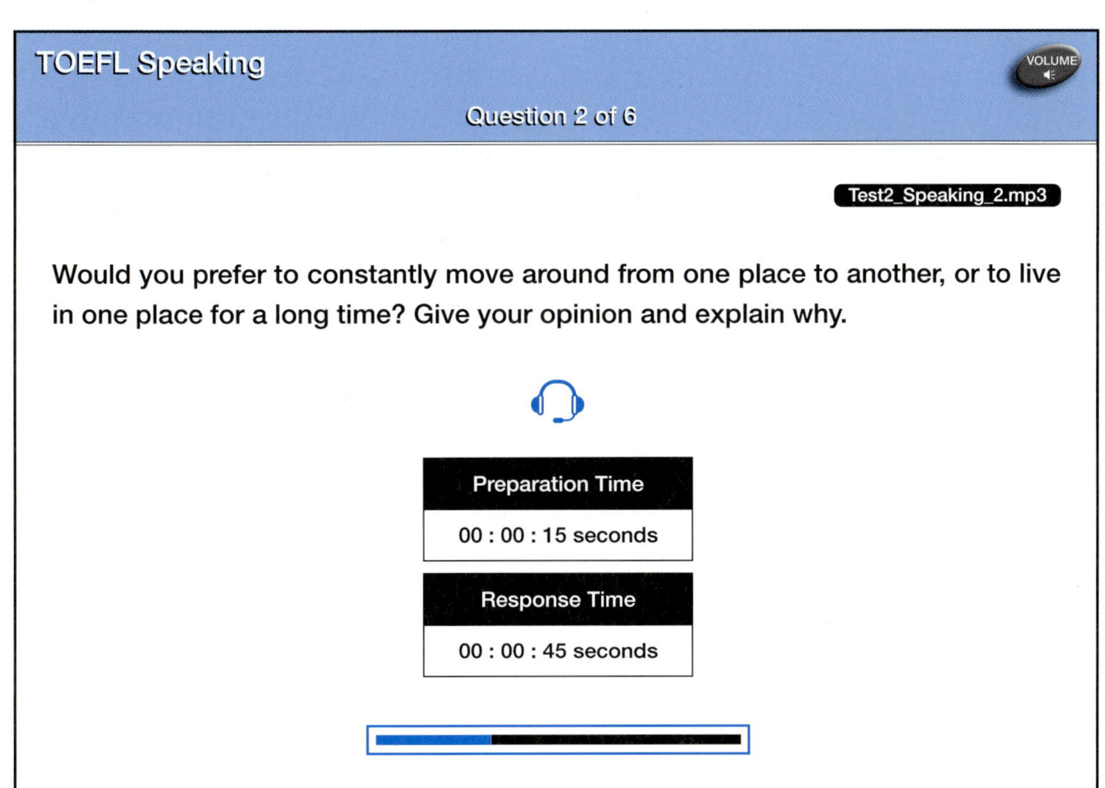
VOLUME
Test2_Speaking_2.mp3
Would you prefer to constantly move around from one place to another, or to live in one place for a long time? Give your opinion and explain why.
Preparation Time
00 : 00 : 15 seconds
Response Time
00 : 00 : 45 seconds

Speaking

Test2_Speaking_3.mp3

Reading Time: 45 seconds

New Policy for Study Abroad Programs in Spain

One of our school's most popular study abroad programs is at Madrid University in Spain. Some changes have been made for this program. As most of you already know, students who studied abroad in Madrid University were guaranteed a dormitory room. However, from now on students will have to find their own housing off campus. The number of students who wish to live on campus has increased at Madrid University, dorms will no longer be prorided for study abroad students. We hope the students consider this change in policy before applying for the study abroad program to Spain.

TOEFL Speaking 

The woman expresses her opinion about the announcement. State her opinion and explain the reasons why she feels that way.

Preparation Time
00 : 00 : 30 seconds

Response Time
00 : 00 : 60 seconds

Test2_Speaking_4.mp3

Reading Time: 45 seconds

Occam's Razor

In the late 1300s and early 1400s, there was a Franciscan monk named William of Occam. Throughout his life, he was part of a number of papal controversies, but these days he is most remembered for a principle called Occam's razor. William of Occam is not the person who created the principle, but he has become famously associated with it because he used it. This principle proposes that if a person is presented with a problem, he should "shave" all unnecessary factors to solve it. Basically, Occam's razor states that the best solution to a problem is usually the simplest solution.

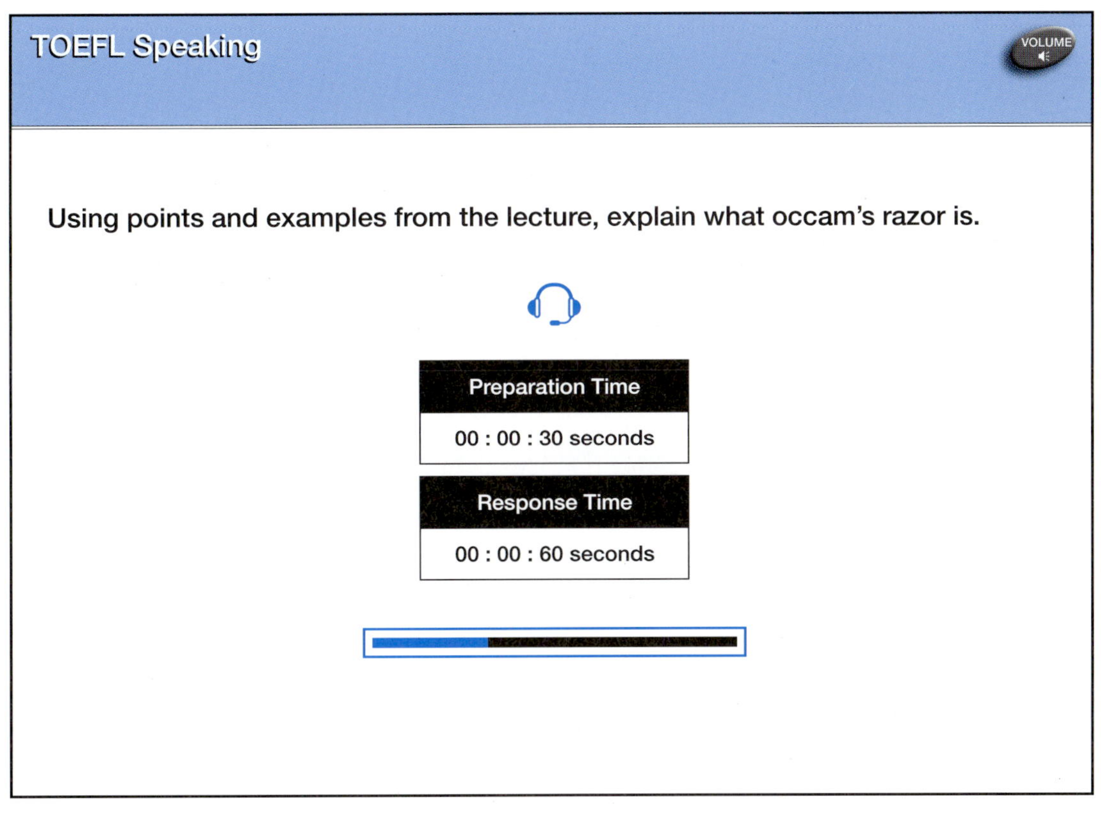

TOEFL Speaking

VOLUME

Using points and examples from the lecture, explain what occam's razor is.

Preparation Time
00 : 00 : 30 seconds

Response Time
00 : 00 : 60 seconds

Speaking

Test2_Speaking_5.mp3

TOEFL Speaking

The woman expresses her feelings about the problem. What is the problem and what are the suggestions that were made? What do you think the woman should do?

Preparation Time
00 : 00 : 20 seconds

Response Time
00 : 00 : 60 seconds

Test2_Speaking_6.mp3

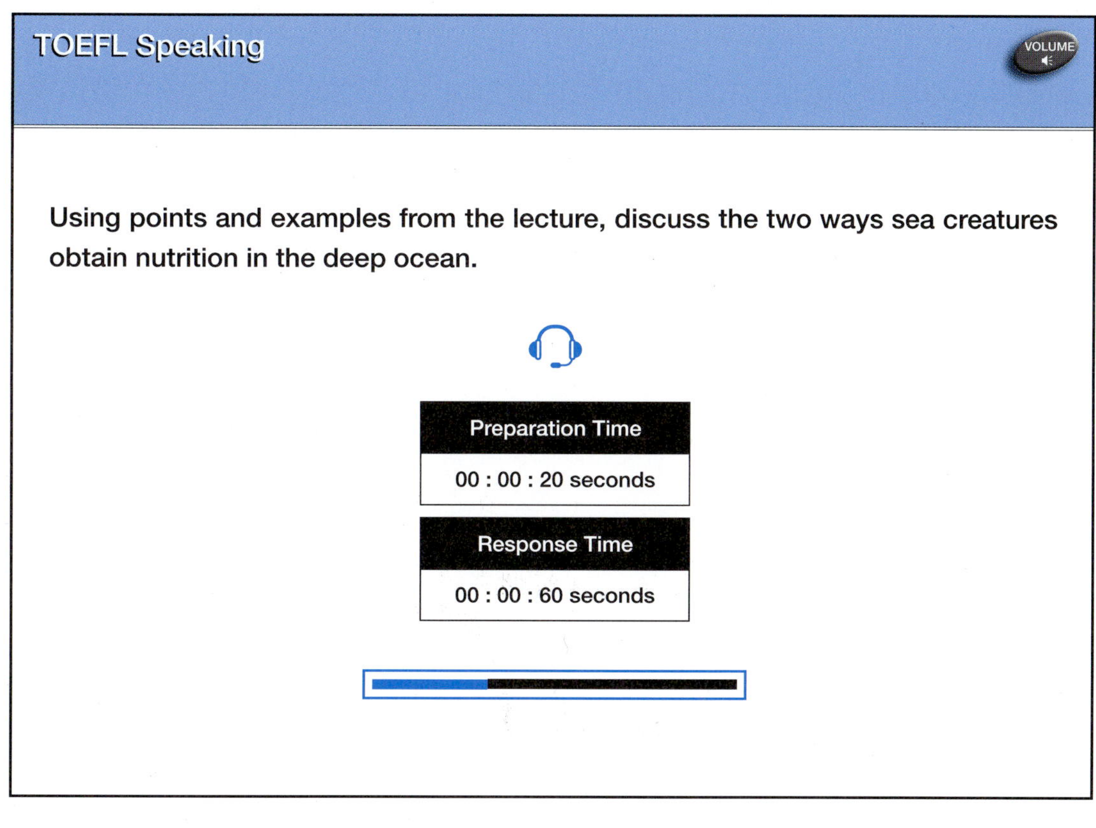

TOEFL Speaking

Using points and examples from the lecture, discuss the two ways sea creatures obtain nutrition in the deep ocean.

Preparation Time

00 : 00 : 20 seconds

Response Time

00 : 00 : 60 seconds

Writing

Writing Section Directions

Be sure your headset is on.

This section measures your ability to write in an academic environment.

There are two tasks in this section. For the first task, there is a reading passage and a lecture. You will write a response to a question based on what you read and hear. For the second task, you will write a response to a question based on your own knowledge and experience.

Now, listen to the directions for the first writing task.

Reading Time: 3 minutes

Recently sugar has been attacked by many health experts who claim that it is unhealthy and causes obesity. However, most foods in industrialized nations today contain large amounts of sugar as consumers prefer the sweet taste. Therefore, there have been recent attempts to create a substance both sweet and healthy. Sucralose is an artificial sweetener created for this; however it has many negative side effects.

This sucralose has been shown to be damaging to the immune system. An experiment with rats shows that this artificial sugar can cause certain organs to shrink. As these organs shrink, the immune system is also weakened leaving the body susceptible to many different kinds of diseases. Large amounts of damage to the immune system can lead to disease and death.

The reason for such damage may be because of the way scientists created this sucralose substance. Sucralose is made by replacing a molecule found in regular sugar with a chemical compound that is poisonous and toxic to most animals and plant life. Although some say that this molecule is harmless, no one knows how this toxic molecule may affect humans in the long run.

Also, this substitute will not solve obesity issues in the end, because people will want more sweet food. As the body naturally craves sugar, there will be natural cravings for people to find foods that have sugar in it. However, since sucralose is not sugar, people will end up eating more sweet foods in an attempt to try and appease the sugar craving. This will lead to more obesity.

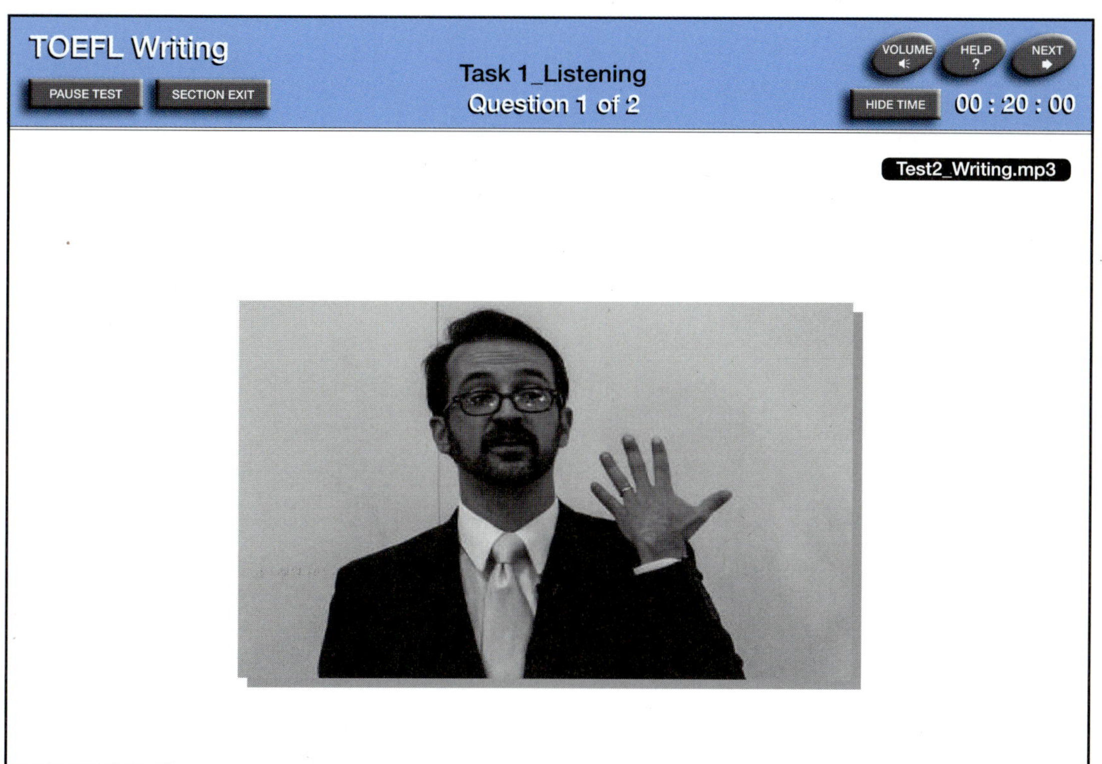

Writing

Note-taking

	Reading	Listening
Main Argument		
Main Point 1		
Main Point 2		
Main Point 3		

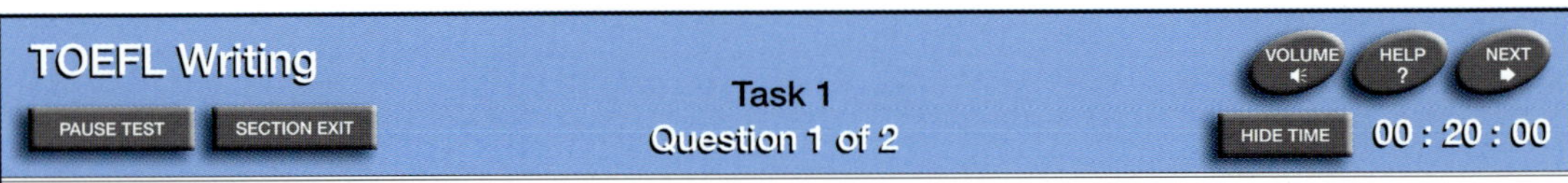

Directions: You have 20 minutes to plan and write your response. Your response will be judged on the basis of the quality of your writing and on how well your response presents the points in the lecture and the relationship to the reading passage. Typically, an effective response will be 150 to 225 words.

Question: Summarize the points made in the lecture, being sure to explain how they cast doubt on specific points made in the reading passage.

TOEFL Writing

PAUSE TEST | SECTION EXIT

Task 2
Question 2 of 2

VOLUME | HELP | NEXT
HIDE TIME 00 : 30 : 00

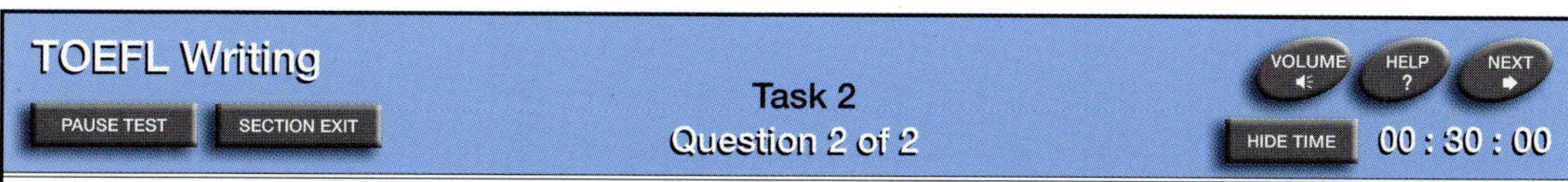

Directions: Read the question below. You have 30 minutes to plan, write, and revise your essay. Typically, an effective response will contain a minimum of 300 words.

Question:

Do you agree or disagree with the following statement?

It is important for the government to provide money to things that are beautiful and not just for things that are practical.

Use specific reasons and examples to support your opinion.

Brainstorming

정답 및 해설

Part 1 Gliding Animals 활공하는 동물들

1. ⓒ	2. Ⓑ	3. Ⓑ	4. Ⓑ	5. ⓒ	6. ⓒ	7. Ⓓ
8. Ⓑ	9. Ⓓ	10. Ⓐ	11. Ⓓ	12. Ⓑ	13. Ⓓ	14. ⓒ, Ⓔ, Ⓕ

1 A myriad of animals have evolved airborne locomotion, either by powered flight or by gliding. While gliding may be a precursor to some forms of powered flight, gliding has some ecological advantages of its own. Gliding is a very energy-efficient way of travelling from tree to tree. Many gliding animals are suggested to eat low energy foods such as leaves and are limited to gliding because of this, whereas flying animals eat more high energy foods such as fruits, nectar, and insects. In contrast to flight, gliding has evolved independently many times among **extant** vertebrates, and these groups have not distributed nearly as much as have groups of flying animals. Gliding, in particular, has evolved among rainforest animals, especially in the rainforests in Asia where the trees are tall and widely spaced. Some animals use gliding as a technique for fleeing from their predators. It allows them to relocate to other trees without touching the ground. It is also known to be efficient in saving their energy when they forage long-distance prey. Gliding animals have been a riveting area of study for scientists. In recent times, scientists discovered that there is a particular prosperity and diversity of gliding animals in Southeast Asia. This recent discovery led the scientists to **come up with** some questions: what is the cause of the biological <u>heterogeneity</u> of the gliding animals discovered in Southeast Asia; how could one analyze the reason for the lack of gliding animals in other regions?; And what makes rain forests in Southeast Asia exceptional?

1 무수히 많은 동물들이 동력 비행 혹은 활공으로 비행 운동능력을 진화시켜왔다. 활공은 동력 비행의 선구자적인 한 형태이며 동시에 특유의 생태학적 이점을 갖기도 한다. 활공은 나무 사이를 옮겨 다니는 에너지 효율적인 방식이다. 많은 활공 동물들은 나뭇잎과 같은 저열량 음식을 섭취하며, 그래서 활공하는 것을 자제한다. 반면 비행하는 동물들은 과일, 넥타, 곤충 등과 같은 고열량 음식들을 섭취한다. 비행과 반대로 활공은 현존하는 척추동물들에 의해 수차례 독립적으로 진화해갔으며, 활공하는 척추동물들은 하늘을 나는 동물들만큼 널리 분포되지 않았다. 특별히 활공은 우림지대 동물들, 특히 나무들이 크고 공간이 넓은 아시아 우림지대의 동물들 사이에서 진화해왔다. 몇몇 동물들은 활공을 천적으로부터 도망치는 기술로 사용해왔다. 활공은 땅을 짚지 않고 한 나무에서 다른 나무들로 옮겨갈 수 있도록 해준다. 또한 멀리 있는 먹이를 찾을 때 에너지를 절약시켜주기도 한다. 활공하는 동물들은 과학자들의 연구영역이 되어왔다. 최근 과학자들은 동남아시아 활공 동물들이 다른 지역에 비해 특별히 더 잘 번성하고 종류도 다양하다는 점을 발견했다. 최근의 이 발견으로 인해 과학자들은 몇 가지 의문점을 가지게 되었다. 첫째, 동남아시아에서 발견된 활공 동물들의 생물학적인 이질성을 유발시키는 것은 무엇인가? 다른 지역에서 활공 동물들이 부족한 이유를 어떻게 분석할 수 있었을까? 그리고 무엇이 동남아시아의 우림지대를 특별하게 만든 것일까?

2 To answer the question of biological heterogeneity of these animals in Southeast Asia, scientists came up with a number of theories. The first theory is often termed the tall-trees hypothesis. The theory suggests that because the trees in Southeast Asia are relatively taller than trees in other regions, the tall trees can offer a resource for longer gliding distances in conjunction with an opportunity to prepare in a dive preceding the gliding. The tallness of Southeast Asian forests is due to the abundance of tropical, lengthy hardwood trees. These trees, with the help of lower wind speeds, accommodate a welcoming environment for gliding, leaving a healthy and diverse environment for gliding animals. Although the tall-trees hypothesis might seem totally accurate, it does contain some notable defects. Firstly, even in the forests in Southeast Asia with shorter trees, which are mainly located in the northern area of the rainforest in China, Thailand, and Vietnam, there exists a diverse environment of gliding animals. Secondly, not all gliders use tall trees to initiate their glides. Some gliders do flourish in low forests, and even metropolitan parks. These show how lengthy trees are not at all necessary for gliding animals. Additionally, countless numbers of gliding animals commence their gliding action at the middle of tree trunks, not climbing to the top of the trees to set off.

3 Second **speculation** is often called the broken-forest hypothesis. **Ecologists speculate that the gliding animals in Southeast Asia jeopardize themselves with descending to the ground or glide to maneuver between trees since the tree canopy contains fewer woody vines that connect the tree crowns compared to the forests in America and Africa.** Also, this theory assumes that the top layer of the forests in Southeast Asia is more asymmetrical in height because of the coexistence of the tall tropical trees and other lower trees. **This** is often beneficial and favored by the gliding animals. It should be

2 동남아시아 활공 동물들의 생물학적 이질성에 대한 질문에 답하기 위해, 과학자들은 몇 가지 이론을 생각해냈다. 첫 번째 이론은 '큰 나무 가설'이라고 불린다. 큰 나무 가설은 동남아시아의 나무가 다른 지역 나무들보다 비교적 키가 크기 때문에 키가 큰 나무들은 활공 전에 급강하할 수 있도록 준비할 기회가 있으므로 더 길게 활공할 수 있는 힘을 제공한다는 것이다. 동남아시아 숲의 나무들이 큰 것은 길고 단단한 열대나무가 많기 때문이다. 이 나무들은 낮은 풍속의 도움으로 활공하기에 알맞은 환경을 제공하며 활공 동물들에게 건강하고 다양한 환경을 제공한다. 큰 나무 가설이 맞아 들어가는 것처럼 보이지만, 이 가설에는 눈에 띄는 모순이 있다. 첫째, 중국, 태국, 베트남의 열대우림 북부지역에 위치한 키 작은 나무들에서도 활공 동물들이 다양한 형태로 발견된다. 둘째, 모든 활공 동물들이 활공을 시작할 때 큰 나무들을 이용하는 것은 아니다. 어떤 활공 동물들은 낮은 농장, 숲, 그리고 심지어 대도시 공원 안에서도 번식한다. 이러한 활공 동물들은 활공 동물들에게 반드시 큰 나무만 필요한 것은 아니라는 것을 보여준다. 게다가 많은 활공 동물들은 활공하기 위해 나무 꼭대기에 오르지 않고 나무줄기 중간에서 활공을 시작한다.

3 두 번째 가설은 종종 '부서진 숲 가설'이라 불린다. 생태학자들은 동남아시아의 활공 동물들이 땅으로 내려가면서 위험에 빠지거나 혹은 나무 사이를 오가기 위해 활공한다고 생각한다. 왜냐하면 미대륙이나 아프리카의 숲과 비교했을 때 나뭇가지들이 지붕 모양으로 우거진 것(tree canopy)은 수관들(tree crowns)을 연결시켜주는 나무 덩굴들이 더 적기 때문이다. 또한 이 이론은 동남아시아 숲의 꼭대기 층이 높이에 있어서 더 비대칭적이다라고 가정하는데 그 이유는 키가 큰 열

noted, however, that ecologists specializing in different regions observed that there is a tremendous local variation in tree height, canopy structure, and abundance of vines depending on various factors including site conditions of soil, slope elevation, climate and local disturbances. Indeed, we can find many locations with abundant woody vines and numerous connections between trees in Southeast Asia and similarly many Amazonian forests with few woody vines.

대 나무들과 다른 키 작은 나무들이 공존하기 때문이다. 이러한 불균형은 종종 활공 동물들에게 이로우며 도움이 된다. 그러나 다른 지역을 연구하는 생태학자들이 토양의 상태, 경사, 기후, 지역적 방해를 포함한 다양한 요소에 따른 덩굴의 양, 그리고 나무의 높이와 나뭇가지 지붕에 있어 지역적인 다양성이 큰 것을 관찰했음을 주목할 필요가 있다. 정말로 우리는 나무 덩굴들이 풍부한 동남아시아의 나무들과 나무 덩굴들이 거의 없는 아마존의 나무들 사이에 연결고리가(연관성이) 많이 있는지 찾을 수 있다.

4 The third theory is unique in that it implies that it is the very existence of tall tropical trees themselves that is sponsoring the evolution of gliding animals. This particular theory claims that forests made up of tall tropical trees may be food deserts for animals living in them. Ⓐ ■ The gliding animals living in tall tropical forests can be classified into two groups: Carnivores that eat small prey such as insects and small vertebrates or leaf eaters. For each group, a tall tropical forest is like a desert in that food resources are few and far apart. For the leaf-eating group, the problem is not the lack of leaves but the lack of edible leaves. Ⓑ ■ In these forests, tall tropical trees account for approximately 50 percent of more of the total number of canopy trees and over 95 percent of large trees. Ⓒ ■ However, their leaves contain high concentration of toxic chemicals, being unavailable to be a reliable food source to a majority of vertebrate plant eaters. Ⓓ ■ **Due to this, most plant eating gliders avoid eating tall tropical leaves, instead travelling widely across the forest to find edible leaves.** The theory suggests that the wide range of travelling across the forest due to the lack of food sources gradually made the animals adopt gliding as a means of navigation since it is more efficient than walking on the ground or jumping between trees. Also, the futility in the number of prey and other insects naturally led various carnivorous animals to

4 세 번째 이론은 독특한데 활공 동물들의 진화를 돕는 것이 바로 키가 큰 열대나무의 존재 그 자체라는 것이다. 이 독특한 이론은 키가 큰 열대 나무로 구성된 숲들이 그곳에 사는 동물들에게는 먹이 없는 사막일 것이라 주장한다. 숲에 사는 동물들은 두 그룹으로 나뉜다. 하나는 곤충이나 작은 초식동물 등을 먹는 육식동물이고 다른 하나는 잎사귀를 먹는 초식동물이다. 각각의 그룹에게, 키가 큰 열대나무 숲은 음식이 거의 없거나 멀리 떨어져 있다는 면에서 사막과 같다. 초식동물들에게는 나뭇잎이 부족한 것이 문제가 아니라 먹을 수 있는 나뭇잎이 부족한 것이 문제가 된다. 이런 숲에서 키가 큰 열대나무가 캐노피 트리(canopy tree)의 거의 50퍼센트 이상을, 큰 나무 중 95퍼센트 이상을 차지한다. 그러나 이 나뭇잎들은 독성 물질을 많이 함유하고 있어서 초식동물들의 주식으로 사용되기는 힘들다. **이 때문에, 대부분의 채식성 활공 동물들은 높이 있는 열대나무의 잎을 먹지 않고, 대신에 먹을 수 있는 잎을 찾기 위해 넓게 돌아다닌다.** 이 이론은 동물들이 먹이 부족으로 숲을 넓게 가로질러 다니다가 먹이 탐색의 수단으로 활공에 점차적으로 적응해갔다고 주장하고 있는데 그 이유는 땅 위를 걷거나 나무 사이를 점프

forage longer distances for their prey. The irregular flowering and fruiting cycles of tall tropical trees cause this paucity of food, represented by the lack of fruits, seeds, flowers, and seedlings that are the starting point of so many food chains. The lack of prey in tall tropical forests affected geckos and lizards to use gliding, which is the most efficient technique, to move between tree crowns to forage for prey.

하는 것보다 활공하는 것이 훨씬 더 효율적이기 때문이다. 또한 먹이와 다른 곤충들의 수가 줄면서 자연스럽게 다양한 육식동물들도 먹이를 사냥하기 위해 더 먼 거리까지 찾아다니게 되었다. 키가 큰 열대 나무의 불규칙한 개화기와 열매 맺기 주기는 많은 먹이 사슬의 시작점이 되는 과일, 씨앗, 꽃, 묘목의 부족으로 대표되는 식량의 부족을 야기한다. 키가 큰 열대 숲 안에서의 먹이 부족은 도마뱀붙이와 도마뱀이 수관과 수관 사이를 이동하며 먹이를 쫓는 데 가장 효과적인 기술인 활공을 이용하도록 만들었다.

어휘_ myriad 무수한 locomotion 이동 gliding 활공 precursor 선구자 efficient 효율적인 vertebrate 척추동물 distribute 분배하다 forage 먹이를 찾다 riveting 매혹적인 heterogeneity 이질성 conjunction 연대 descend 하강하다 coexistence 공존 abundant 풍부한 futility 무익 paucity 결핍

---

1. According to the paragraph 1, which of the following is inferred about the flight or flying animals?
   Ⓐ Flight is related to low energy food.
   Ⓑ Flying animal is an ancestor of gliding animal.
   Ⓒ Flying animals have distributed in various places.
   Ⓓ Gliding is less energy efficient way than flying.

단락 1에 따르면, 다음 중 비행동물들에 대해 알 수 있는 것은 무엇인가?
   Ⓐ 비행은 저열량 음식과 관련되어 있다.
   Ⓑ 비행 동물은 활공 동물의 조상이다.
   Ⓒ 비행 동물은 다양한 곳에 분포되어 있다.
   Ⓓ 활공은 비행보다 덜 에너지 효율적이다.

2. In paragraph 1, the word extant is closest in meaning to
   Ⓐ available
   Ⓑ remaining
   Ⓒ died
   Ⓓ prevailing

지문의 extant와 가장 가까운 의미를 지닌 단어는?
   Ⓐ 가능한
   Ⓑ 남아 있는
   Ⓒ 죽은
   Ⓓ 우세한

3. In paragraph 1, the word **come up with** is closest in meaning to

Ⓐ contribute to

Ⓑ conceive

Ⓒ be aware of

Ⓓ avoid

지문의 **come up with**와 가장 가까운 의미를 지닌 단어는?

Ⓐ 기여하다

Ⓑ 생각하다

Ⓒ ~에 주의하다

Ⓓ 피하다

4. What is the reason for the ability to glide being considered useful to forest-dwelling species in paragraph 1?

Ⓐ Because gliding serves as a rapid, energy efficient way of descending from trees

Ⓑ Because gliding provides an advantage of moving through the forest without being exposal to predators in the ground

Ⓒ Because gliding helps animals to adapt to various forests conditions

Ⓓ Because gliding enables moving short distances in foraging for food

단락 1에서, 숲에 사는 종들에게 활공하는 능력이 유용하다고 생각되는 이유가 무엇인가?

Ⓐ 활공이 빠르고, 에너지 효율적으로 나무에서 내려오도록 해주기 때문에

Ⓑ 활공이 땅에서 적들에게 노출되지 않고 숲을 돌아다니게 해주는 이점을 제공하기 때문에

Ⓒ 활공이 동물들이 다양한 숲 상황에 적응하도록 도와주기 때문에

Ⓓ 활공이 음식을 찾기 위해 짧은 거리를 이동하도록 해주기 때문에

5. The author includes the last sentence in paragraph 1 in order to

Ⓐ provide examples showing that there were many different types of animals

Ⓑ describe events leading up to the events in the following paragraphs

Ⓒ announce the organization of the passage

Ⓓ present a concluding idea to summarize paragraph 1

저자는 단락 1의 마지막 문장을 ~ 위해 포함한다.

Ⓐ 많은 다른 종류의 동물들이 있다는 것을 보여주는 예를 제공하기

Ⓑ 다음 단락들에서 사건을 이끄는 사건을 묘사하기

Ⓒ 지문의 구성을 알려주기

Ⓓ 단락 1을 요약하는 결론을 보여주기

6. Which of the following does NOT support the tall-trees hypothesis in paragraph 2?

Ⓐ Lengthy trees enable longer glide range.

Ⓑ Tall trees enable to prepare in a dive.

Ⓒ There are hostile environments to populate gliding animals.

Ⓓ There is lower wind speed between tall trees.

다음 중 무엇이 단락 2의 큰 나무 가설을 지지하지 않는가?

Ⓐ 긴 나무들은 더 긴 활공 범위를 가능하게 해준다.

Ⓑ 큰 나무들은 낙하를 준비하는 것을 가능하게 해준다.

Ⓒ 활공 동물들이 살 수 있는 적대적 환경이 있다.

Ⓓ 키가 큰 나무들 사이에는 풍속이 낮다.

7. **Which of the following is the defect in the tall-trees hypothesis in paragraph 2?**
   Ⓐ Gliding animals are evenly spread throughout the forests of the Southeast Asian region.
   Ⓑ Most gliding animals are incapable of climbing to the tops of trees.
   Ⓒ Many gliding animals cannot start their glides in short trees.
   Ⓓ Many gliding animals are discovered in forests where trees tend to be relatively shorter.

다음 중 무엇이 단락 2의 큰 나무 가설의 결점인가?
   Ⓐ 활공 동물은 동남아시아 지역의 숲에 균일하게 분포되어 있다.
   Ⓑ 대부분의 활공 동물들은 나무 꼭대기까지 오르는 능력이 없다.
   Ⓒ 많은 활공 동물들은 작은 나무에서 활공을 시작할 수 없다.
   Ⓓ 많은 활공 동물들이 나무들이 상대적으로 키가 작은 경향이 있는 숲에서 발견된다.

8. **The word speculation is closest in meaning to**
   Ⓐ argument
   Ⓑ thought
   Ⓒ question
   Ⓓ examination

지문의 speculation와 가장 가까운 의미를 지닌 단어는?
   Ⓐ 주장
   Ⓑ 생각
   Ⓒ 질문
   Ⓓ 조사

9. **The word jeopardize is closest in meaning to**
   Ⓐ imply
   Ⓑ initiate
   Ⓒ appreciate
   Ⓓ imperil

지문의 jeopardize와 가장 가까운 의미를 지닌 단어는?
   Ⓐ 암시하다
   Ⓑ 시작하다
   Ⓒ 감사하다
   Ⓓ 위태롭게 하다

10. **In paragraph 3, the word This refers to**
   Ⓐ Imbalance of trees' height
   Ⓑ Speculation
   Ⓒ Tall trees
   Ⓓ Short trees

단락 3에서, This가 지시하는 것은
   Ⓐ 나무 높이의 불균형
   Ⓑ 추측
   Ⓒ 높은 나무
   Ⓓ 짧은 나무

11. Which of the sentences below best expresses the essential information in the highlighted statement in the passage? *Incorrect answer choices change the meaning in important ways or leave out essential information.*

Ⓐ Ecologists thought that in forests with an uneven canopy structure, gliding is difficult and animals moved to other places where the trees are all about the same height.

Ⓑ Ecologists in other regions have found that gliding animals are as flourishing and heterogeneous in some forests of Africa and America as they are in Southeast Asian forests.

Ⓒ Ecologists have thought that gliding animals are not found in areas of Southeast Asia where trees are connected by vines.

Ⓓ Ecologists have thought that with the fewer woody vines connecting the tops of trees, gliding animals in Southeast Asia are in danger or move between trees.

아래의 문장들 중 지문에서 강조된 문장의 필수 정보를 가장 잘 표현한 문장은 어느 것인가? *잘못된 선택지는 중요한 의미를 바꾸거나 핵심 정보를 생략하고 있다.*

Ⓐ 생태학자들은 불균등한 나뭇가지 지붕 구조의 숲에서는 활공이 어렵고 동물들이 나무들의 높이가 비슷한 곳으로 옮겨간다고 생각했다.

Ⓑ 다른 지역의 생태학자들은 활공하는 동물이 동남아시아의 숲에서 그렇듯이 몇몇 아프리카와 미국의 숲에서 번성하고 이질적이라는 것을 찾았다.

Ⓒ 생태학자들은 나무들이 덩굴로 연결되어 있는 동남아시아지역에서는 활공 동물을 찾을 수 없다고 생각했다.

Ⓓ 생태학자들은 나무 꼭대기를 잇는 덩굴이 더 적게 있는 동남아시아의 숲들에 있는 활공 동물은 위험에 빠지거나 나무 사이로 이동한다고 생각했다.

12. According to paragraph 4, what problem do leaf-eating animals face in forests with tall tropical trees?

Ⓐ There is no efficient method of obtaining leaves from trees.

Ⓑ Trees that have edible leaves are spread out.

Ⓒ Leaves of most trees are located very high, making animals difficult to reach.

Ⓓ The tall tropical trees have less leaves than those of other canopy trees.

단락 4에 따르면, 키가 큰 열대나무가 있는 숲에서 잎을 주식으로 하는 동물들은 어떤 문제에 직면하는가?

Ⓐ 나무로부터 잎을 얻는 효과적인 방법이 없다.

Ⓑ 먹을 수 있는 잎을 가진 나무들이 퍼져 있다.

Ⓒ 대부분의 나무들의 잎은 매우 높게 위치해 있고, 동물들이 닿기 힘들게 만든다.

Ⓓ 높은 열대 나무들은 다른 캐노피트리들에 비해 더 적은 잎을 가지고 있다.

13. Look at the four squares [■] that indicate where the following sentence could be added to the passage.

Due to this, most plant eating gliders avoid eating tall tropical leaves, instead travelling widely across the forest to find edible leaves.

Where would the sentence best fit?

다음의 문장이 지문에 추가될 수 있도록 하는 4개의 사각형을 보라.

이 때문에, 대부분의 채식성 활공 동물들은 높이 있는 열대나무의 잎을 먹지 않고, 대신에 먹을 수 있는 잎을 찾기 위해 넓게 돌아다닌다.

문장이 어디에 가장 적절히 들어가겠는가?

14. Directions: An introductory sentence for a brief summary of the passage is provided below. Complete the summary by selecting the **THREE** answer choices that express the most important ideas in the passage. Some sentences do not belong in the summary because they express ideas that are not presented in the passage or are minor ideas in the passage. **This question is worth 2 points.**

Various theories have been suggested to explain the unique abundance and diversity of gliding animals in the rain forests of Southeast Asia.

-
-
-

Ⓐ The very fact that gliding animals are most ample and flourishing in the forests with short trees represents that gliding did not evolve as an adaptation to an environment of tall trees.

Ⓑ The abundance of gliding animals in different parts of the world corresponds to difference in tree heights.

Ⓒ One view argues that various gliding species have evolved so extensively in Southeast Asia since the forests have been particularly tall; however, the theory remains insufficient.

Ⓓ Jumping from tree to tree or walking in forests that are dominated by tall trees may be less energy consuming compared to gliding.

Ⓔ The tall tropical trees create an environment where most species travel extensively to find food, and gliding may have evolved as a rapid and efficient way of relocating between tree crowns.

Ⓕ The hypothesis that gliding evolved to compensate for a paucity of vines linking tree canopies overlooks the problematic evidence from both Southeast Asian and Amazonian forests.

지문의 간단한 요약의 도입문장이 아래에 제공되어 있다. 지문에서 중요한 생각을 나타내는 3가지 정답을 선택해서 요약문을 완성하라. 몇몇 문장은 요약에 포함되지 않는데 왜냐하면 지문에 나타나지 않거나 중요하지 않은 생각이기 때문이다. 이 문항은 2점이다.

다양한 이론들이 동남아시아의 열대우림에 있는 활공 동물들의 독특한 풍부함과 다양성을 설명하기 위해 제안되었다.

-
-
-

Ⓐ 활공하는 동물들이 키 작은 나무를 가진 숲에서 가장 많고 번영한다는 사실은 활공이 키 큰 나무의 환경에 대한 적응으로써 진화한 것이 아니라는 것을 보여준다.

Ⓑ 세계의 다른 지역에서의 활공 동물의 풍부함은 나무 높이의 차이와 부합한다.

Ⓒ 하나의 관점은 숲들이 특히 높았기 때문에 다양한 활공 동물 종들이 동남아시아에서 광범위하게 진화하였다고 주장한다; 하지만, 그 이론은 불충분한 채로 남았다.

Ⓓ 나무에서 나무로 뛰어다니거나, 높은 나무들이 많은 숲에서 걸어 다니는 것은 활공하는 것에 비해 덜 에너지 소모적일 수 있다.

Ⓔ 높은 열대나무들은 대부분의 종들이 음식을 찾기 위해 넓게 돌아다녀야 하는 환경을 만들고, 활공은 나무들 사이를 효과적이고 빠르게 돌아다니도록 하는 방법으로써 진화했을 것이다.

Ⓕ 활공이 캐노피나무를 연결하는 덩굴의 결핍에 대한 보상으로써 진화했다는 가설은 동남아시아와 아마존 숲에서 나온 문제가 제기되는 증거를 간과한다.

1. Ⓑ	2. Ⓑ	3. Ⓓ	4. Ⓒ	5. Ⓒ	6. Ⓒ	7. Ⓐ
8. Ⓐ	9. Ⓓ	10. Ⓒ	11. Ⓒ	12. Ⓓ	13. Ⓐ	14. Ⓒ, Ⓓ, Ⓔ

1 Sumer was one of the ancient civilizations and historical regions during the Early Bronze Age. The first civilization could be found along the Tigris and Euphrates rivers in the land, which is now Iraq. It is **fascinating** how these lands were settled by people because there were a variety of challenges that make the area difficult to live in. For example, there were basically little natural resources that the civilization could rely on such as timber or ore. In addition to **this**, rainfall throughout the year was neither constant nor stable due to limited amounts of precipitation and annual floods originated from snow in nearby mountains. Riverbeds were also constantly shifted. Subsequently, this required irrigation system and water channeling to be developed to ensure survival. **As the irrigation system grew to be reliable and the flow of water was controlled, large areas with many people emerged with complex cultures and organization, erecting massive buildings and temples**. As a result, a privileged class emerged to organize these irrigation systems which gained and held power by controlling the dispersal of extra crops.

1 수메르는 고대 문명사회 중 하나이며 초기 청동시대 유적지 중 하나이다. 첫 번째 문명은 지금의 이라크 지역에 있는 티그리스(Tigris)강과 유프라테스(Euphrates)강을 따라 발견되었다. 어떻게 이 지대에 사람들이 정착하게 되었는지 놀라울 따름인데 그 이유는 이 지대가 사람이 살기에는 많이 힘든 곳이기 때문이다. 예를 들어, 문명이 발달하는 데 필요한 목재나 광석과 같은 천연 자원이 기본적으로 거의 없었다. 게다가 제한적인 연간 강수량과 인근 산의 눈에서 기원하는 연례 홍수로 인해 연중 강수량이 일정하거나 안정되지도 않았다. 강바닥 또한 끊임없이 이동되었다. 그 결과, 사람들은 살아남기 위해 관개 시설과 수로의 발달을 필요로 하게 되었다. 관개 시설이 안정적으로 발달하고 물의 흐름을 조절할 수 있게 되면서 거대한 건물들과 사원들이 세워졌고 인구가 많은 넓은 지역들에는 복잡한 문화와 조직이 생겨났다. 그 결과, 특권층은 추가 작물들의 분산을 통제할 수 있는 힘을 갖는 이러한 관개 시설들을 체계화하기 시작했다.

2 There is an **assumption** that various cities emerged in this area. Examples for such cities can be seen in Eridu and Uruk. The first settlement in southern Mesopotamia was established at Eridu, by farmers who brought with them the Hadji Muhammed culture, which first pioneered irrigation agriculture. This culture was derived from the Samarran culture of northern Mesopotamia. Eridu remained an important religious center when it was gradually surpassed in size by the **adjacent** city of Uruk. The leaders

2 다양한 도시들이 이 지역에 나타났다는 가정이 있다. 그러한 도시들의 예는 에리두와 우르크에서 볼 수 있다. 남 메소포타미아의 첫 정착은 에리두에서 이루어졌는데, 관개 농업의 선구자 역할을 한 핫지 무하메드 문화(Hadji Muhammed culture)를 들여온 농부들이 그 주인공들이었다. 이 문화는 북 메소포타미아의 사마라 문화에서 유래되었다. 우르크의 인접 도시에 의해 점차 크기가 커지면서 에

and privileged populations of these cities believed that they somehow had relations to the gods, and believed that they were protected by their own respective patron god or gods.

3 Sumerian had a distinctive style of fine quality painted pottery which spread throughout Mesopotamia and the Persian Gulf. It appears that this early culture was a combination of three distinct cultural influences: peasant farmers, living in wattle and daub or clay brick houses and practicing irrigation agriculture; hunter-fishermen living in woven reed houses and living on floating islands in the marshes (Proto-Sumerians); and Proto-Akkadian nomadic pastoralists, living in black tents.

4 In addition, the first form of writing emerged in this area as the civilization became sophisticated, advanced and organized. Deciphered syllabary writing system was developed, which has allowed archaeologists to read contemporary records and inscriptions. Sumerians engraved symbols into damp tablets of clay to write. The name of these symbols that represented words or objects was known as logograms. The Sumerian probably used written characters for the purpose of maintaining inventories of livestock and merchandise as well as literature and theology with most other early alphabets of the time.

리두는 종교의 중요한 중심지로 남게 되었다. 이 도시들의 지도자들과 특권층은 어찌되었든 간에 자신들이 신들과 관련되어 있고 각각의 고유한 수호신과 기타 다른 신들에 의해 보호받고 있다고 믿었다.

3 수메르인들은 메소포타미아와 페르시아 만에 걸쳐 퍼진 독특한 스타일의 고품질 채문토기를 가지고 있었다. 그들의 초기 문화는 세 가지 뚜렷한 문화적 영향의 결합을 보여주는데, 윗가지에 흙벽을 발라 만든 집 또는 진흙 벽돌 집에 살면서 관개 농업을 하는 소작농들, 그리고 갈대로 지은 집과 습지의 떠다니는 섬에 사는 사냥하는 어부들(최초의 수메르인들, Proto-Sumerians), 마지막으로 검은 텐트 안에 사는 최초의 아카드 유목민들(Proto-Akkadian nomadic pastoralist)이 그것들이다.

4 그리고 문명으로서 이 지역 최초의 글의 형태는 정교해졌고 고급스러워졌으며 조직화되었다. 판독된 음절문자체계 문자는 잘 발달되어 있었고, 고고학자들이 동시대의 기록들과 명문들을 읽을 수 있게 해주었다. 수메르인들은 기호들을 딱딱하지 않은 흑판에 새겼다. 말과 사물을 표현하는 이 기호들의 이름은 어표로 알려져 있다. 수메르인들은 아마도 가축과 물품의 재고자산과 그 당시 대부분의 초기 알파벳들로 이루어진 문학과 신학체계뿐 아니라 가축과 상품의 목록을 보존하기 위한 목적으로 글자를 사용했을 것이다.

어휘_ bronze age 청동기시대 timber 목재 ore 광석 precipitation 강수 irrigation system 관개시설 erect 세우다 agriculture 농업 peasant 소작농의 hunter-fishermen 수렵 채집민 nomadic 방랑하는 pastoralist 목축민 sophisticated 복잡한 contemporary 동시대의 predominately 지배적으로, 대부분

---

1. The word fascinating in the passage is closest in meaning to
   Ⓐ consistent
   Ⓑ interesting
   Ⓒ equivalent
   Ⓓ fictional

지문의 fascinating과 가장 가까운 의미를 지닌 단어는?
   Ⓐ 일관된
   Ⓑ 흥미로운
   Ⓒ 동등한
   Ⓓ 허구의

2. The word this in the passage refers to
   Ⓐ timber or ore
   Ⓑ lack of natural resources
   Ⓒ settlement in Tigris and Euphrates rivers
   Ⓓ unstable precipitation

지문에서 this가 나타내고 있는 것은?
   Ⓐ 목재나 광석
   Ⓑ 천연자원의 부족
   Ⓒ 티그리스와 유프라테스 강에서의 정착
   Ⓓ 불안정한 강수

3. Why does the author mention 'fascinating' in the passage?
   Ⓐ To show that the land was qualified to populate
   Ⓑ To exaggerate that the area was populated by a limited number of people
   Ⓒ To show that the land was an ideal condition
   Ⓓ To demonstrate that the area was not the suitable area to live in but people settled in the area

저자가 지문에서 fascinating을 언급한 이유는?
   Ⓐ 그 지역이 거주하기에 적절하다는 것을 보여주기 위해
   Ⓑ 그 지역은 거주자의 수가 제한되어 있었다는 것을 과장하기 위해
   Ⓒ 그 지역이 이상적인 상황이었다는 것을 보여주기 위해
   Ⓓ 그 지역이 살아가기에 적절한 지역은 아니었지만 사람들이 정착했다는 것을 입증하기 위해

4. According to paragraph 1, which of the following
was NOT difficulty that the lands along the Tigris and
Euphrates River had?
   Ⓐ The deficiency of natural resources
   Ⓑ Low amounts of precipitation
   Ⓒ Droughts caused by limited amount of snow
   Ⓓ Thawing snow causing annual flooding

단락 1에 따르면, 티그리스와 유프라테스강을
따라 있는 지역들에 있던 어려움이 아닌 것은
무엇인가?
   Ⓐ 천연자원들의 부족
   Ⓑ 적은 강수
   Ⓒ 제한된 눈의 양으로 인한 가뭄
   Ⓓ 해동된 눈으로 인한 연례적인 홍수

5. Which of the sentences below best expresses the
essential information in the highlighted statement
in the passage? *Incorrect answer choices change
the meaning in important ways or leave out essential
information.*
   Ⓐ The increase of capricious giant new cities
   depended on the ability to control the flow of water
   via irrigation system in order to build impressive
   structures.
   Ⓑ After the flow of water was controlled, the irrigation
   system was responsible for the rise of new cities
   with large population that erected numerous
   temples and buildings.
   Ⓒ As the irrigation system developed and was able
   to direct the course of water, it became viable for
   large areas to develop and could develop cultures
   and organization.
   Ⓓ Taking control of the flow of water with developed
   culture facilitated the growth of impressive temples
   and buildings.

아래의 문장들 중 지문에서 강조된 문장의 필수
정보를 가장 잘 표현한 문장은 어느 것인가? *잘
못된 선택지는 중요한 의미를 바꾸거나 핵심 정
보를 생략하고 있다.*
   Ⓐ 변화가 심하고 거대한 새 도시의 증가는 인
   상적인 구조를 만들기 위해 물 흐름의 조절
   과 관개 시설에 의존하였다.
   Ⓑ 물의 흐름을 제어할 수 있게 된 후, 관개 시
   설은 수많은 사원과 건물을 세운 거대한 규
   모의 새로운 도시 생성의 원인이 되었다.
   Ⓒ 관개 시설이 발달하고 물의 경로를 조절할
   수 있게 되면서, 넓은 지역이 발달하고 문
   화와 구조를 발전시킬 수 있었다.
   Ⓓ 발달된 문화에서 물의 흐름을 제어하는 것
   은 인상적인 사원과 건물의 발전을 촉진시
   켰다.

6. The word assumption in the passage is closest in
meaning to
   Ⓐ composition
   Ⓑ aggression
   Ⓒ postulation
   Ⓓ scrutiny

지문의 assumption과 가장 가까운 의미를 지
닌 단어는?
   Ⓐ 구성
   Ⓑ 공격
   Ⓒ 가정
   Ⓓ 조사

7. The word adjacent in the passage is closest in
   meaning to
   Ⓐ neighboring
   Ⓑ distinctive
   Ⓒ acute
   Ⓓ remote

지문의 adjacent와 가장 가까운 의미를 지닌
단어는?
Ⓐ 이웃하는
Ⓑ 독특한
Ⓒ 심각한
Ⓓ 외딴

8. In paragraph 2, why does the author mention the city
   of Eridu?
   Ⓐ To exemplify the first settlement by farmers
   Ⓑ To illustrate the simplicity of the culture
   Ⓒ To compare characteristics of Eridu with those of
      Uruk
   Ⓓ To elaborate on the reason why the city was
      developed

단락 2에서 저자가 도시 에리두에 대하여 언급
한 이유는?
Ⓐ 농부들의 첫 정착의 예시를 들기 위하여
Ⓑ 문화의 단순성을 표현하기 위하여
Ⓒ 에리두와 우르크의 특성을 비교하기 위하여
Ⓓ 도시가 발달한 이유에 대해 설명하기 위하여

9. According to paragraph 3, which of the following is
   NOT true about components of early culture?
   Ⓐ Wandering people
   Ⓑ Practicing irrigation agriculture
   Ⓒ Peasant farmers
   Ⓓ Building the house

단락 3에 의하면 초기 문화의 구성요소들에 관
해 사실이 아닌 것은?
Ⓐ 방랑하는 사람들
Ⓑ 사냥하는 사람들
Ⓒ 소작 농부들
Ⓓ 정교한 빌딩

10. According to paragraph 4, Sumerian writing systems
    are NOT used for the purpose of
    Ⓐ theology
    Ⓑ management of supply of livestock and products
    Ⓒ engraving letters
    Ⓓ literature

단락 4에 의하면 수메르의 문자 체계는 다음의
목적으로 쓰이지 않았다
Ⓐ 신학
Ⓑ 가축과 제품의 공급에 대한 관리
Ⓒ 문자를 새기는 것
Ⓓ 문학

11. According to paragraph 4, what made Sumerian writing system invented?

Ⓐ A refined administration process

Ⓑ Process-oriented management

Ⓒ Increased complexity of organization in cities

Ⓓ Authority figures

단락 4에 의하면 무엇이 수메르인들이 문자를 만들도록 하였는가?

Ⓐ 정제된 관리 과정

Ⓑ 과정에 기인한 경영

Ⓒ 도시에서의 구조 복잡화 증가

Ⓓ 권위자들

12. According to paragraph 5, which of the following is true about the wheel?

Ⓐ The origin of the wheel is equivocal.

Ⓑ A more important impact was gained through the use of the wheel in transportation.

Ⓒ It is unclear whether the wheel was meant for pottery since it was used for transportation around the same time.

Ⓓ The use in transportation was not the first purpose.

단락 5에 의하면, 바퀴에 관해서 무엇이 사실인가?

Ⓐ 바퀴의 유래는 모호하다.

Ⓑ 운송에 있어서 바퀴의 사용으로 인해 더 중요한 영향이 생겼다.

Ⓒ 거의 비슷한 시기에 운송에 사용되었기 때문에 바퀴가 그릇으로 이용이 되었는지는 불명확하다.

Ⓓ 운송수단에서의 사용이 첫 목적이 아니었다.

13. According to paragraph 5, what can be inferred about farming tool before 2900 BCE?

Ⓐ Bronze tools were not used in farming and war.

Ⓑ Sumerian didn't use stone and copper tools.

Ⓒ With an outside culture, the Sumerians learned how to create bronze.

Ⓓ Before the Sumerians had learned it the skill had been achieved in other societies.

단락 5에 의하면, 기원전 2900년 이전의 농업 도구들에 대해서 무엇이 추론될 수 있는가?

Ⓐ 청동 도구들은 농업과 전쟁에 쓰이지 않았다.

Ⓑ 수메르인들은 돌과 구리 도구를 사용하지 않았다.

Ⓒ 외부 문화와 함께, 수메르인들은 청동을 만드는 법을 배웠다.

Ⓓ 수메르인들이 배우기 전에 그 기술은 이미 다른 사회에서 성취되었다.

14. Direction: An introductory sentence for a brief summary of the passage is provided below. Complete the summary by selecting the **THREE** answer choices that express the most important ideas in the passage. Some sentences do not belong in the summary because they express ideas that are not presented in the passage or are minor ideas in the passage. **This question is worth 2 points.**

지문의 간단한 요약의 도입문장이 아래에 제공되어 있다. 지문에서 중요한 생각을 나타내는 3가지 정답을 선택해서 요약문을 완성하라. 몇몇 문장은 요약에 포함되지 않는데 왜냐하면 지문에 나타나지 않거나 중요하지 않은 생각이기 때문이다. 이 문항은 2점이다.

The first permanent groups that settled along the Tigris and Euphrates rivers successfully overcame many challenges.

티그리스와 유프라테스 강을 따라 영구적으로 정착한 첫 정착 무리는 많은 어려움을 성공적으로 극복했다.

-
-
-

Ⓐ The social structure of cities were highly divided and held the belief that they were protected through their own respective patron deities.

Ⓑ One particular city of Uruk was unique in that it was protected by two patron gods instead of the typical singular god.

Ⓒ A writing system over time developed that gained efficiency to use a various kinds of areas.

Ⓓ Irrigation system and control of water flow was one of the crucial constituents to develop cities with organization and culture.

Ⓔ Additional breakthrough of this society was the wheel and the invention of bronze, which allowed superior aspects for farming tools and weapons.

Ⓕ Although this society eventually figured out how to make bronze, the skill was not unsurpassed by neighboring cultures.

Ⓐ 도시의 사회적인 구조는 잘 나누어져 있었고 그들 자신이 그들만의 신들로부터 보호받는다는 믿음을 가지고 있었다.

Ⓑ 우르크라는 특정 도시는 하나의 신이 아니라 두 신들로부터 보호받는다는 것에 있어서 독특했다.

Ⓒ 시간이 지남에 따라 발달된 문자체계는 다양한 종류의 지역에서 효율성을 주었다.

Ⓓ 관개 시설과 물의 흐름의 조정은 도시의 구조와 문화를 발달시키는 것에 있어 중요한 구성요소 중 하나였다.

Ⓔ 이 사회에서의 획기적 사건은 바퀴와 청동의 발명이었는데, 이것은 농업도구와 무기에서 우월한 측면을 가능하게 해주었다.

Ⓕ 이 사회가 결국 청동을 만드는 법을 파악했지만, 그 기술은 이웃하는 문화를 넘지 못했다.

Part 3 Portrait 초상화

1. Ⓑ	2. Ⓒ	3. Ⓓ	4. Ⓓ	5. Ⓓ	6. Ⓓ	7. Ⓐ
8. Ⓓ	9. Ⓑ	10. Ⓒ	11. Ⓒ	12. Ⓓ	13. Ⓓ	14. Ⓑ, Ⓒ, Ⓔ

1 Portrait is referred to as a representation or delineation of a person, especially of the face by drawing, painting, photography, and engraving. The purpose of portrait is to display the likeness, personality, and even the mood of the person. Yet, definition like this neglects to capture the sophistication of portrait. Portraits are the products of art that are related to the notions of the character as they are recognized, characterized, and inferred in different eras and regions, **rather than** to directly try to capture the superficial counterpart. These notions of the character may incorporate gender, age, profession, social hierarchy, and the character of the subject, among other things. Instead of being static, these characteristics are representative of the assumptions and circumstances of the period when the portrait was contrived. It is unattainable to duplicate the notions of characters; it is only possible to evoke or advise them. Therefore, although portraits depict individuals, the artists stress on the conventional or **stock** types of the subjects rather than their unique qualities. Portrait has also been exposed to constant changes in practice and artistic convention but portraits are still product of prevailing artistic fashions and favored styles, techniques, and media. Consequently, it can be said that portrait encompasses an ample amount of art category that provides a wide range of interactions with psychological, social, and artistic practices and assumptions.

1 초상화는 데생, 그림, 사진, 판화 등의 방법으로, 특히 사람의 얼굴을 묘사하는 것이라고 정의되어 있다. 초상화법은 닮은 모습, 성격, 심지어 기분까지도 표현해 내는 데 그 목적이 있다. 하지만 이러한 정의는 초상화의 정교함을 잡아내지 못한다. 초상화는 표면적인 상대를 잡아내려는 직접적 시도를 한다기보다 다른 시대와 지역에서 인정받고 특징지어지고 추론되는 인물의 관념과 연관되는 예술작품이다. 이러한 인물의 관념은 다른 것들 사이에서 성별, 나이, 직업, 사회적 지위, 그리고 대상의 성격을 통합할 수도 있다. 비교적 정적인 대신에, 이 특징들은 그 초상화가 그려진 시대의 가정과 상황을 대표한다. 그것은 인물의 관념을 복사해서 얻어질 수 있는 것이 아니며, 오직 그들을 환기시키거나 도움을 주어야만 한다. 그러므로 비록 초상화가 개개인을 묘사했다고는 하나 예술가들은 그들의 독특한 특징들보다는 좀 더 전통적인 대상의 평판 등을 더 중요하게 여긴다. 또한 초상화 예술은 관습과 예술적인 전통 속에서 끊임없는 변화에 노출되어왔지만 여전히 예술적 유행과 대중이 선호하는 스타일, 테크닉, 미디어가 지배하는 산물일 것이다. 따라서 초상화 예술은 심리적, 사회적, 그리고 예술적 관행과 추측과의 넓은 범위의 상호작용을 제공하는 충분한 양의 예술 카테고리를 망라한다고 볼 수 있다.

2 Considering that portraits are different from other genres or art categories in their crafting method, the content, and the use, they are worthy of being separately studied. Ⓐ ▪ First, the production of portraits requires the presence of an individual or their image in most cases. Ⓑ ▪ Therefore, the production of portraits accompanies the interaction between the subject and the artist since it requires them to see each other eye to eye. Ⓒ ▪ If the subject is of nobility or is busy and unavailable to be in the studio routinely, artists could also use photographs or sketches to finish their portraits. Ⓓ ▪ **Occasionally, portrait artists should have direct or indirect relationships with their subjects.** During the 17th and 18th centuries in Europe, sitting times were occasionally reduced due to focusing solely on the head and then employing professional drapery painters to complete the painting. For example, an **English artist** had with him a series of sketches containing various poses that enable him to solely focus on the head and to lessen the sitting time of the aristocrats. Portrait painter could also be asked to depict the similarities of individuals who were the deceased. For these instances, painters used prints or photographs of the subject to reproduce the image. **Hypothetically**, portraits could work from the memories or feelings when creating a painting, but this is a rare occurrence according to documented records. Nevertheless, the course of crafting a portrait is intimately associated with the implicit or explicit participation of the model whether it be model sittings, copying a photograph or sketch, or using memory.

2 초상화가 제작 방법, 내용, 용도에서 다른 장르나 다른 예술 카테고리들과 차별되는 것을 고려해보면 초상화는 독자적으로 연구될 가치가 있다. 첫째, 초상화 제작은 대부분의 경우 한 개인의 참석이나 그들의 이미지를 요구한다. 그러므로 초상화 제작은 대상과 예술가 사이의 상호작용이 동반되어야 하는데 그 이유는 대상과 예술가가 서로 눈을 마주쳐야 하기 때문이다. 만일 대상이 너무 귀족층이거나 바빠서 작업실에 정기적으로 오기 힘든 경우 예술가는 초상화를 완성하기 위해 사진이나 밑그림을 이용할 수도 있다. **때때로, 초상화가들은 그들의 대상과 직접적이거나 간접적인 관계를 가져야만 했다.** 17~18세기 유럽에서는 앉아 있는 시간이 종종 줄어들었는데 그 이유는 오직 머리 부분에만 초점을 맞추어서 전문적인 휘장 화가들이 그림을 완성하도록 시켰다. 하나의 예시로, 영국의 예술가는 다양한 포즈가 담긴 일련의 스케치를 가지고 있었는데 그 때문에 그는 대상의 머리 부분에만 신경 쓸 수 있었고 귀족들이 앉아 있는 시간을 줄일 수 있었다. 초상화가는 이미 세상을 떠난 사람들을 비슷하게 그려달라는 요청도 받기도 했다. 한 예로 화가들은 (죽은) 대상의 이미지를 다시 만들어내기 위해서 인쇄물이나 사진을 이용했다. 가정해보자면 초상화는 그림이 그려질 당시의 기억이나 느낌으로부터 그려지기 시작한다. 하지만 이것은 문서화된 기록에 따르면 어쩌다 있는 일이다. 그럼에도 불구하고 초상화를 그리는 과정은 앉아 있는 모델이건, 사진이나 스케치를 카피하건 아니면 기억을 이용하건 간에 숨어 있거나 드러나 있는 모델의 참여와 밀접하게 연관되어 있다.

3 Not to mention, portrait can be set apart from other artistic genres such as still life, landscape, and history by its relevance with appearance, or likeness. Consequently, the genre of portrait received its disapproval for copying instead of for artistic originality or inspiration; therefore portrait is sometimes viewed as inferior to other artistic genres. This notion is well shown in the Renaissance art theory, where portrait became associated with the degree of **cursory** imitation as opposed to fine art, which was linked with originality and inspiration. One of the examples of the prevailing attitude towards portrait is Michelangelo's renowned objection to painting portrait, not having ideally beautiful models to portrait. Satirically, many made their living through portrait. During the 19th and 20th centuries when modernism prevailed, the reception towards portrait was critical. Portrait maintained to survive despite its theoretical criticisms. For example, Picasso became well known for his cubist stilllife drawings in his initial career, but some of the most impressive experiments in this new style were his portraits of art dealers.

3 물론 초상화는 외모나 유사성과 관련되어 있기 때문에 멈춰 있는 생명, 풍경, 그리고 역사와 같은 다른 예술적 장르들과는 구분된다. 그 결과 초상화라는 장르는 장르의 독창성이나 영감 대신에 복사라는 반감을 샀다. 그래서 초상화는 때로 다른 예술장르보다 열등한 대접도 받았다. 이러한 생각은 (19세기 초까지 지배했었던) 르네상스 예술 이론에 잘 나타나 있는데, 초상화는 독창성 및 창의성과 연관되어 있는 순수예술에 반하는 피상적 모방 정도로 취급받았다. 초상화에 대해 지배적인 태도를 보여주는 한 예로 미켈란젤로가 그릴 만한 아름다운 모델들이 없다며 초상화를 그리지 말자고 반대했다는 유명한 일화를 들 수 있다. 아이러니컬하게도 많은 사람들이 초상화를 통해 생계를 이었다. 모더니즘이 만연하던 19~20세기에는 초상화가 비판적으로 받아들여졌다. 초상화는 이론적 비판에도 불구하고 여전히 존재했다. 예를 들어, 피카소는 그의 초기 작품인 자신의 입체파 정물화로 유명해졌지만, 이 새로운 스타일에서 가장 인상적인 실험들은 미술상들을 그린 그의 초상화들이었다.

어휘_ delineation 묘사 engraving 판화 neglect 무시하다 sophistication 복잡성 superficial 피상적인 incorporate 포함하다 hierarchy 계급제도 static 정적인 assumption 가정 contrive 고안해내다 evoke 일깨우다 convention 관습 prevailing 우세한 accompany 동반하다 nobility 귀족 depict 묘사하다 inferior 열등한 satirically 풍자적으로

1. The word rather than is closest in meaning to
  Ⓐ despite
  Ⓑ instead of
  Ⓒ in addition to
  Ⓓ related to

2. According to paragraph 1, which of the following is NOT true about portrait?
  Ⓐ It includes drawing, painting, photography, and engraving.
  Ⓑ Its goal is to describe the likeness, personality and the attitude of a person.
  Ⓒ It describes the superficial character.
  Ⓓ The definition of the word is sometimes inadequate to describe portrait.

3. The word stock is closest in meaning to
  Ⓐ apparent
  Ⓑ distinct
  Ⓒ steady
  Ⓓ typical

4. According to paragraph 1, which of the following accurately depicts the development of portrait?
  Ⓐ It became more popular after starting as a secondary art form.
  Ⓑ Due to its static manner, it is a relatively more stable art form.
  Ⓒ It is the very first art form concerned with the personality of the model.
  Ⓓ It has undergone consistent major style shifts.

5. According to paragraph 2, what is true of the differences between portrait and other types of art?
  Ⓐ Portraits require a collaboration of multiple artists.
  Ⓑ Portraits more accurately portray the subject than other forms of art.
  Ⓒ Portraits require less time to produce than other art forms.
  Ⓓ Portraits require some level of personal interaction between the artist and the subject compared to other art forms.

지문의 단어 rather than과 가장 가까운 의미를 지닌 단어는?
  Ⓐ ~에도 불구하고
  Ⓑ ~ 대신에
  Ⓒ ~에 추가로
  Ⓓ ~와 관련된

단락 1에 따르면, 다음 중 무엇이 초상화에 대해 사실이 아닌가?
  Ⓐ 그것은 그림, 묘사, 사진, 또는 판화 등을 포함한다.
  Ⓑ 그것의 목적은 사람의 닮음, 성격, 그리고 태도를 묘사하는 것이었다.
  Ⓒ 그것은 피상적인 특성을 묘사한다.
  Ⓓ 단어의 정의는 때때로 초상화를 묘사하기에 불충분하다.

지문의 단어 stock과 가장 가까운 의미를 지닌 단어는?
  Ⓐ 명백한
  Ⓑ 뚜렷한
  Ⓒ 지속적인
  Ⓓ 전형적인

단락 1에 따르면, 다음 중 초상화의 발전을 가장 정확하게 묘사하는 것은?
  Ⓐ 2차적 미술 형식으로 시작된 후로 더욱 인기 있어졌다.
  Ⓑ 그것의 정적인 특성 때문에, 그것은 상대적으로 더 안정적인 미술 형식이다.
  Ⓒ 그것은 모델의 성격과 연관된 첫 미술 형식이다.
  Ⓓ 그것은 꾸준히 주요한 스타일 변화를 겪었다.

단락 2에 따르면, 다음 중 초상화와 다른 종류의 미술의 차이점에 대해 사실인 것은?
  Ⓐ 초상화는 다수의 미술가들의 협동을 요구한다.
  Ⓑ 초상화는 다른 형식의 미술보다 대상을 더 정확하게 나타낸다.
  Ⓒ 초상화는 다른 형태의 미술보다 만드는 데 더 적은 시간을 요구한다.
  Ⓓ 초상화는 다른 형태의 미술에 비해 미술가와 대상 사이의 어느 정도의 개인적인 상호작용을 요구한다.

6. The word Hypothetically is closest in meaning to
   Ⓐ Primarily
   Ⓑ Particularly
   Ⓒ Directly
   Ⓓ Theoretically

지문의 단어 Hypothetically와 가장 가까운 의미를 지닌 단어는?
Ⓐ 우선
Ⓑ 특히
Ⓒ 직접적으로
Ⓓ 이론적으로

7. In paragraph 2 why does the author mention an English artist?
   Ⓐ To present an example of an artist who adopted a practice in order to reduce the necessary time of sittings of aristocrats
   Ⓑ To show used the help of professional drapery artists to help him finish his portraits
   Ⓒ To represent it focuses on painting varying body parts of the subject at each sitting
   Ⓓ To show it have a wide range of patrons as subjects

단락 2에서 저자가 영국 예술가를 언급한 이유는?
Ⓐ 귀족들이 앉아 있어야 하는 시간을 줄이기 위한 방법을 적용한 미술가의 예를 보여주기 위해
Ⓑ 그의 초상화를 마치기 위해 전문적 휘장 화가들을 고용한 것을 보여주기 위해
Ⓒ 각각의 자세에서 몸의 다른 부분에 집중한 그림을 대표한다는 것을 보여주기 위해
Ⓓ 넓은 범위의 고객을 대상으로 가졌다는 것을 보여주기 위해

8. In paragraph 2, what is NOT mentioned as methods used by painters to create portraits
   Ⓐ Directly observing the subjects during a sitting
   Ⓑ Copying a photograph
   Ⓒ Using memory to elicit how the subject looked like
   Ⓓ Combining traits from a number of subjects

단락 2에서, 다음 중 화가들이 초상화를 만들기 위해 사용한 방법으로 언급되지 않은 것은?
Ⓐ 앉은 자리에서 정확히 대상을 관찰하는 것
Ⓑ 사진을 따라서 그리는 것
Ⓒ 대상이 어떻게 생겼는지를 이끌어내기 위해 기억을 사용하는 것
Ⓓ 몇 개의 대상으로부터 특성을 조합하는 것

9. According to paragraph 3, portrait is viewed as being of a lower status because of
   Ⓐ innovation
   Ⓑ copy
   Ⓒ perfectionism
   Ⓓ creativity

단락 3에 따르면, 초상화는 다음의 이유 때문에 더 낮은 지위에 있는 것으로 보인다
Ⓐ 혁신
Ⓑ 복사
Ⓒ 완벽주의
Ⓓ 창의성

10. The word cursory is closest in meaning to
   Ⓐ misunderstanding
   Ⓑ famous
   Ⓒ superficial
   Ⓓ insignificant

지문의 단어 cursory와 가장 가까운 의미를 지닌 단어는?
Ⓐ 오해
Ⓑ 유명한
Ⓒ 피상적인
Ⓓ 중요하지 않은

11. According to paragraph 3, what can be inferred about Michelangelo's view of portrait?

    Ⓐ He believed that imitation was a requirement for creativity.

    Ⓑ He felt that portrait art should be examined as a form of fine art.

    Ⓒ He believed that portraits should portray idealized beauty.

    Ⓓ He thought that subjects should rather be from the ancient times than contemporary.

단락 3에 따르면, 다음 중 초상화에 대한 미켈란젤로의 관점에 대해 추론될 수 있는 것은?

    Ⓐ 그는 창의성을 위해 모방이 요구된다고 믿었다.

    Ⓑ 그는 초상화가 순수미술의 형태로 보여야 한다고 느꼈다.

    Ⓒ 그는 초상화가 이상화된 미를 묘사해야 한다고 믿었다.

    Ⓓ 그는 대상이 동시대보다는 고대의 것이어야 한다고 생각했다.

12. The author in paragraph 3 discusses Picasso as an example of an artist who

    Ⓐ modified the way other artists felt about portrait art

    Ⓑ relied solely on portrait to rise to fame

    Ⓒ had scarcely any theoretical opposition to portrait than most modern artists

    Ⓓ drew portraits despite his doubts about portrait being a fine art form

단락 3에서 저자는 피카소를 다음과 같은 화가에 대한 예로 보여주기 위해 언급했다

    Ⓐ 다른 화가들이 초상미술에 대해 느끼는 것을 변화시킨 화가

    Ⓑ 유명해지기 위해 초상화에만 의존한 화가

    Ⓒ 대부분의 현대 미술가에 비해 초상화에 대한 이론적인 반대를 거의 하지 않은 화가

    Ⓓ 초상화가 순수미술의 형태라는 것에 대한 의심에도 불구하고 초상화를 그린 화가

13. Look at the four squares [▪] that indicate where the following sentence could be added to the passage

Occasionally, portrait artists should have direct or indirect relationships with their subjects.

Where would the sentence best fit?

다음의 문장이 지문에 추가 될 수 있도록 하는 4개의 사각형을 보라.

때때로, 초상화가들은 그들의 대상과 직접적이거나 간접적인 관계를 가져야만 했다.

문장이 어디에 가장 적절히 들어가겠는가?

14. Directions: An introductory sentence for a brief summary of the passage is listed below. Complete the summary by selecting the **THREE** answer choices that most accurately depicts the most important ideas in the passage. Some sentences do not belong in the summary because they express ideas that are not presented in the passage or are minor ideas in the passage. **The question is worth 2 points.**

Portrait as an art form is more complex than is suggest by its definition.

-
-
-

Ⓐ The dictionary has consistently changed the definition of portrait art throughout the years to manifest the shifting attitudes regarding the genre.

Ⓑ Portrait art should be classified as a unique artistic genre due to its relation with the subject and the way in which it was formed.

Ⓒ Portrait art was at times viewed negatively since it was characterized as simple copying, lacking of artistic originality.

Ⓓ Starting in the Renaissance and continuing into the start of the nineteenth century, portrait art was admired to a greater extent than it is today.

Ⓔ Portraits generally represent the conventions of the time rather than the distinct qualities of the individual.

Ⓕ Majority of artists throughout history avoided portrait art since it was regarded as a mechanical art form.

지문의 간단한 요약의 도입 문장이 아래에 제공되어 있다. 지문에서 중요한 생각을 나타내는 3가지 정답을 선택해서 요약문을 완성하라. 몇몇 문장은 요약에 포함되지 않는데 왜냐하면 지문에 나타나지 않거나 중요하지 않은 생각이기 때문이다. 이 문항은 2점이다.

미술 형식으로서의 초상화는 그것의 정의에 나타난 것보다 복잡하다.

-
-
-

Ⓐ 사전은 장르에 따라 바뀌는 태도를 분명히 나타내기 위해 초상화의 정의를 지속적으로 몇 해에 거쳐 바꾸었다.

Ⓑ 초상화는 대상과의 긴밀한 교류와 그것이 형성되는 방법 때문에 독자적인 미술 장르로 분류되어야 한다.

Ⓒ 초상화는 예술적 독창성이 없는 상태로 그저 단순한 복제로 특징지어져 부정적으로 보일 때가 있었다.

Ⓓ 르네상스에 시작하여 19세기의 시작 무렵까지 지속적으로, 초상 미술은 오늘날보다 더 대단한 정도로 열망되었다.

Ⓔ 초상화들은 일반적으로 개인의 뚜렷한 특성보다는 시대의 관습을 대표하였다.

Ⓕ 역사를 통틀어 대부분의 미술가들은 그것이 기술적인 미술 형태로 여겨졌기 때문에 초상화를 피했다.

Part 1   Questions 1-5

1. Ⓑ   2. Ⓑ   3. Ⓐ, Ⓑ   4. Ⓒ   5. Ⓒ

[Questions 1-5] Listen to part of a conversation between a student and a professor.
학생과 교수님의 대화 일부분을 들으시오.

Test2_Listening_Part1_01-05.mp3

S   I apologize for being late, Professor Mills, I just came all the way from the student infirmary. I twisted my ankle during soccer practice today and it took some time to get it seen by the doc.

P   That's fine, it's not a problem, David. I just went through your paper on the political philosophies of John Dewey and there were some issues that I wanted to go over with you. First of all, you did a nice job with the biographical information in the opening. However, as you mentioned his political philosophy, I think you could have done a better job organizing his philosophy within the contemporary context. By that I mean, you should have associated Dewey's philosophy with other philosophers of the era.

S   You mean I didn't talk about the kind of influences that he could have received from other intellectuals?

P   Exactly! Take a look at this part here, where you described Dewey's opinion of individuality. I like the context of the information. However, you could have presented this information in a more meaningful manner. For instance, you could have presented this information right after this paragraph on Dewey's ideological influences from other philosophers. You could also add some comments from other scholars related to the issue.

S   늦어서 죄송해요, 밀스 교수님. 학교 양호실에서 여기로 방금 왔어요. 오늘 축구 연습하는 데 발목을 삐었거든요. 의사와 약속 잡는 데 시간이 좀 걸렸어요.

P   괜찮아. 문제 없어, 데이비드. 존 듀이의 정치철학에 관한 보고서를 보았고, 몇 가지 논의하고 싶은 게 있어. 우선 시작 부분에 전기 내용을 집어넣은 건 잘했어. 그런데 정치철학에 대해 언급한 부분은 시대적인 맥락 안에서 철학을 구성하는 게 좀 더 나은 내용을 만들 수 있을 거라고 생각해. 그 시대의 다른 철학자들과 듀이의 철학을 관련짓는 게 좋다는 말이지.

S   교수님께서 말씀하시는 게 제가 그가 다른 지식인들에게 받은 영향들을 말하지 않았다는 거지요.

P   맞아. 여기 이 부분에서 듀이의 의견을 개별적으로 묘사했어. 나는 이 내용이 좋아. 하지만, 너는 이 정보를 더 의미 있게 표현할 수도 있었지. 예를 들어 다른 철학자들로부터 듀이가 받은 사상적인 영향을 쓴 문단 바로 뒤에 이 정보를 집어넣을 수 있었을 거야. 또한 이 주제와 관련된 다른 학자들의 몇 개의 논평을 집어넣을 수도 있고.

S You mean this paragraph?
P Yes. For example, when you finished writing your essay did you revise it to see if all the contents of the essay were relevant to each other?

S Well, not really.
P You see you could have cut out some of the unnecessary information. What I am trying to say is that you needed to organize all this content in a logical order. It's a little hard to understand what direction your essay is heading.

S Whoa. It seems like I've got a lot to revise.
P Here is your work that you should go through. Afterwards, revise and edit it again. As for me, I always edit my work after I finish writing. Most professional writers usually end up removing a lot of their work. You should consider that. Another thing, can you access a copy of the department's guidelines for index and reference citations?

S I checked out the online version when I was writing this essay.
P I think you should print out a copy of it and really pay attention to it for all of your political science papers. I think you were a little confused with the citation rules.

S Sorry, my high school had a different set of rules and I guess I wasn't used to using a new index system.
P I understand. You need to keep in mind that, as an academic convention, you really should stick to a specific set of rules that I ask you to use. Well… That's that… Now, do you think you will be attending this Saturday's political science club meeting?

S Well, as long as I'm alive, I will be there. I heard the discussion will be on John Dewey.

S 이 문단을 말씀하시는 거지요?
P 그래. 에세이를 완성하고 나서, 에세이를 교정하고 모든 내용이 다 서로 관련이 있는지를 확인했니?

S 아니요.
P 여기 몇 개의 불필요한 정보들을 없애야 해. 내가 말하고 싶은 것은 모든 정보들을 논리적인 순서에 맞게 구성해야 한다는 거야. 네 에세이가 어느 방향으로 가는지 이해하는 게 약간 힘들거든.

S 후, 고쳐야 할 것들이 많아 보이네요.
P 여기 네 글이 있으니까 꼼꼼하게 훑어보는 게 좋겠어. 그리고 고치고 다시 편집해. 나도 글을 다 쓴 후에 항상 편집을 하거든. 그리고 대부분의 전문 작가들도 보통 작품의 많은 부분들을 지우게 되더라. 그런 것에 대해 생각해 봐야 해. 또 다른 것으로는, 참조문과 참고문헌 인용에 관한 학과지침에 접속할 수 있니?

S 이 에세이를 쓸 때 온라인 버전을 확인했어요.
P 우선 그것을 프린트하고, 모든 정치과학 보고서에 확실히 적용시켜야 해. 내 생각에 네가 인용 규칙을 잘 모르는 거 같아.

S 죄송해요. 제가 고등학교 때는 다른 규칙들을 사용해서, 새로운 시스템에 익숙하지 않았나 봐요.
P 이해해. 학문적인 관례로서 내가 사용하라고 요청한 구체적인 규칙을 따라야 한다는 것을 기억할 필요가 있어. 그래, 그건 그렇고, 토요일 정치과학 클럽 모임에 참여할 수 있니?

S 제가 살아 있는 한 반드시 갈게요. 토론이 존 듀이에 관한 거라고 들었어요.

P We needed a discussion leader for the meeting and I was wondering if you would be interested in such a role. Tom Hayward asked for someone to take the responsibility. I think you have enough knowledge about Dewey and I thought you could maybe participate and contribute.

S Definitely! It sounds like fun, I'll make sure to talk to Tom.

P 모임의 토론 사회자가 필요해서 그러는데 혹시 네가 그 역할에 관심이 있는지 모르겠다. 톰 헤이워드가 그 임무를 맡아줄 사람이 있는지 물어보더라. 내가 생각으로는 네가 듀이에 관해 충분한 지식이 있으니, 아마 모임에 참석해서 기여를 할 수 있을 거야.

S 그렇고말고요. 재밌을 거 같네요. 제가 톰에게 얘기할게요.

어휘_ infirmary 병원, 양호실 contemporary 동시대의, 현대의 intellectuals 지식인들 ideological 사상적인 citation 인용

---

1. Why does the man go to the professor's office ?

Ⓐ To apologize that he was late at the meeting due to a doctor's appointment

Ⓑ To receive the professor's feedback and reaction on his essay

Ⓒ To discuss John Dewey's philosophy with the professor

Ⓓ To ask about the political science meeting on John Dewey

남자는 왜 교수 사무실에 갔는가?

Ⓐ 의사의 약속 때문에 미팅에 늦은 것을 사과하기 위해

Ⓑ 그의 에세이에 대한 교수의 피드백과 반응을 받기 위해

Ⓒ 교수와 존 듀이의 철학을 논의하기 위해

Ⓓ 존 듀이에 대한 정치과학 미팅에 대해 물어보기 위해

Listen again to a part of the conversation. Then answer the question.
대화의 일부분을 듣고 질문에 답하시오.

Here is your work that you should go through. Afterwards, revise and edit it again. As for me, I always edit my work after I finish writing. Most professional writers usually end up removing a lot of their work. You should consider that.

여기 네 글이 있으니까 꼼꼼하게 훑어보는 게 좋겠어. 그리고 고치고 다시 편집해. 나도 글을 다 쓴 후에 항상 편집을 하거든. 그리고 대부분의 전문 작가들도 보통 작품의 많은 부분들을 지우게 되더라. 그런 것에 대해 생각해봐야 해.

---

2. Why does the professor say this: 🎧 As for me, I always edit my work after I finish writing

Ⓐ To indicate that her own writing needs a lot of editing

Ⓑ To imply that it's necessary for the student to edit his writing

교수는 왜 이것을 말하는가? 나도 글을 다 쓴 후에 항상 편집을 하거든.

Ⓐ 그녀의 글이 많은 편집을 필요로 하다는 것을 알려주기 위해

Ⓑ 학생이 그의 글을 편집할 필요가 있다는 것을 암시하기 위해

© To imply that the student's work is not good to submit

© 학생의 작품이 제출하기에 충분하지 않다는 것을 암시하기 위해

© To contrast the student's tendency to edit before writing

© 글쓰기 전에 편집을 하는 학생의 성향에 반대하기 위해

3. **What are the two technical flaws that the professor point out in the student's essay? Click on 2 answers.**

학생의 에세이에서 교수가 지적한 두 가지 기술적인 결함은 무엇인가? **정답을 두 개 클릭하시오.**

Ⓐ The essay could be presented in a more logical order.

Ⓐ 에세이는 좀 더 논리적인 순서로 표현되어야 한다.

Ⓑ The essay contains irrelevant information that could be cut out.

Ⓑ 에세이는 삭제될 수 있는 관련 없는 정보를 포함하고 있다.

Ⓒ The essay did not include the biographical information of John Dewey.

Ⓒ 에세이는 존 듀이의 전기적인 정보를 포함하지 않았다.

Ⓓ The essay is not organized in chronological order.

Ⓓ 에세이는 시대적인 순서로 구성되어 있지 않다.

4. **Why does the professor recommend the student to lead the discussion for the political science club meeting?**

교수는 학생을 왜 정치과학 클럽 모임에서 토론 사회자로 추천했는가?

Ⓐ The student needs to help Tom Hayward who does not know anything about John Dewey.

Ⓐ 학생은 존 듀이에 대해서 아무것도 모르는 톰 헤이워드를 도울 필요가 있다.

Ⓑ The student can receive help revising his essay on John Dewey.

Ⓑ 학생은 존 듀이에 대한 그의 에세이를 수정하는 데 도움을 받을 수 있다.

Ⓒ The student might be qualified for discussing the topic.

Ⓒ 학생은 주제에 대한 논의에 적격일 수 있다.

Ⓓ The student wants to learn more about John Dewey in order to write a better essay on him.

Ⓓ 학생은 더 좋은 에세이를 쓰기 위해서 존 듀이에 대해 더 많이 배우길 원한다.

Listen again to a part of the conversation. Then answer the question.
대화의 일부분을 듣고 질문에 답하시오.

P Now, do you think you will be attending this Saturday's political science club meeting?

S Well, as long as I'm alive, I will be there.

P 토요일 정치과학 클럽 모임에 참여할 수 있니?

S 반드시 갈게요. 토론이 존 듀이에 관한 거라고 들었어요.

5. **What does the student mean when he says:** 🎧 **Well, as long as I'm alive, I will be there.**

학생이 다음과 같이 말할 때 무엇을 의미하는가?: 제가 살아 있는 한 반드시 갈게요.

Ⓐ The student will attend the meeting if he heals from his injuries.

Ⓐ 학생은 상처에서 나으면 모임에 참석할 것이다.

Ⓑ The student wants to receive a good score on his papers.

Ⓒ The student will make sure to attend the meeting.

Ⓓ The student realizes that attending the meeting will leave a good impression with the professor.

Ⓑ 학생은 보고서에서 좋은 성적을 받기를 원한다.

Ⓒ 학생은 확실히 모임에 참석할 것이다.

Ⓓ 학생은 모임에 참석하는 것이 교수에서 좋은 인상을 남길 것이라는 것을 안다.

Part 1　Questions 6-11

6. Ⓒ　　**7.** Ⓒ　　**8.** Ⓑ　　**9.** Ⓓ,　　**10.** Ⓒ, Ⓓ, Ⓔ　　**11.** Ⓒ

[Questions 6-11] Listen to part of a lecture in an archeology class.
고고학 수업의 강의 일부분을 들으시오.

Test2_Listening_Part1_06-11.mp3

Today, I want to start by talking about excavation, an essential part of archaeology. What do you think excavation is? Most of us have a vague idea about excavation, perhaps that it's digging a site continuously until something valuable is found. This, in reality, is actually a popular myth. Although a little luck is helpful, we get more help from our array of highly sophisticated devices that raise our efficiency. By that I mean it would be a waste of time and energy if we were to dig a site randomly, hoping to somehow strike an ancient structure. One of these recently developed tools, called a muon detector, was actually created by a different field of study. This machine, which can be seen as interdisciplinary, resulted from the application of particle physics.

First, I should explain what a muon is. It is a charged elementary particle, much like an electron. On the Earth, most naturally occurring muons are created by cosmic rays. Cosmic rays consist mostly of protons, many of which arrive from deep space and are highly energized. When cosmic rays, consisting of charged particles, collide with molecules in the upper atmosphere

오늘, 저는 고고학의 중요한 부분인 발굴에 관한 이야기로 시작하고 싶군요. 여러분은 발굴이 무엇이라고 생각하십니까? 우리 대부분은 고고학에 대해서 모호한 개념만을 알고 있습니다. 무언가 값진 것이 나올 때까지 끊임없이 어떤 장소를 파는 것이라고요. 하지만, 이것은 그냥 대중적이며 근거 없는 이야기에 불과합니다. 조금의 행운이 도움이 될지 몰라도, 우리는 일의 효율을 높여주는 매우 복잡한 기계들로부터 더 많은 도움을 받습니다. 제 말은, 만약 우리가 어떻게든 유적을 발견하기를 바라면서 아무 곳이나 파본다면, 그것은 시간과 에너지를 낭비하는 일이란 거죠. 이러한 도구들 중 뮤온탐지기로 부르는 비교적 최근에 발전된 도구는 사실상 다른 분야의 연구로부터 만들어졌습니다. 여러 학문의 분야가 연관된 것으로 보일 수 있는 이 기계는 분자 물리학의 응용에서 기인하였습니다.

우선, 저는 뮤온이 무엇인지 설명하겠습니다. 뮤온은 전자와 많이 비슷한 하전 소립자입니다. 지구에서 자연적으로 생겨나는 뮤온은 대부분 우주선(線)에서 만들어지지요. 우주선은 거의 양성자들로 구성되어 있습니다. 이 양성자들은 먼 우주로부터 왔고 매우 강력한 힘을 가집니다. 이 충전된 우주선이 위쪽 대기권에 있는 입자들과 충돌할 때 그들은 작은 입자들로 분해됩니다. 이

they disintegrate into smaller particles. These small particles are called muons, okay? Archeologists are interested in muons because they have an intriguing property. Muons, which travel at the speed of light, can penetrate tens of meters into rocks and other matter on the Earth's surface. This means that they can pass through solid matter and transmit deep into the surface, which is very useful for archeologists studying buried historical sites.

You see, when a detector takes several months and builds up a picture showing the shadows of a historical structure, archeologists wonder if there are buried chambers or other rooms inside. Think of the Colosseum in Rome, as an example. In cases like this, a muon detector releases a great number of muons passing through the less dense space inside the Colosseum. To go into more detail about this process you need to be aware that muons passing through dense material, such as stone walls, lose energy. From this, obviously, you can expect muons moving through void space to lose less energy and to be present in greater numbers. The muon detector comes into use here to identify the area by measuring the amount of muons in each place. When there are relatively many particles the detector will indicate the space as empty with darker colors.

Afterwards, we are left with a sort of picture of the site and its internal structure. It's not too hard to understand, especially if you already know how CT scans produce a 3-D picture of your body using x-rays. In the medical sense it's really similar to tomography. Now, with the muon detector, we can see what's inside a structure before we dig up the site. This is practical, because we can minimize the damage by excavating only the parts we need to. Since even a little damage can mean losing crucial information forever, archeologists have to be very careful.

작은 입자들을 바로 뮤온이라고 부릅니다. 고고학자들은 뮤온이 흥미로운 특징을 가지고 있기 때문에 관심이 많습니다. 빛의 속도로 이동하는 뮤온은 지각의 다른 물질들은 물론 바위를 수십 미터까지 뚫을 수 있습니다. 이것은 그것들이 단단한 물질을 지나갈 수 있고 표면 아래 깊숙한 곳까지 침투할 수 있다는 말입니다. 이런 특징은 고고학자들이 묻혀 있는 역사적 장소들을 연구하는 데 매우 도움이 됩니다.

탐사기가 몇 달에 걸려서 역사적 구조물의 아웃라인을 만들어내면, 고고학자들은 그 안에 숨어 있는 방이나 다른 공간들이 있는지 상상하죠. 예를 들어, 로마에 있는 콜로세움을 생각해봅시다. 이러한 경우, 뮤온탐지기가 콜로세움 안에 밀도가 낮은 공간을 통과할 수 있는 많은 수의 뮤온을 방출합니다. 이 과정을 더 자세하게 설명하자면, 여러분은 콜로세움 바위벽과 같은 밀집된 물체를 통과하는 뮤온은 에너지를 잃는다는 것을 알고 있어야 합니다. 그럼, 상대적으로 빈 공간을 지나갈 때 뮤온들이 에너지 손실이 덜하고 많은 양이 감지되는 것을 예상할 수 있죠. 이때 뮤온탐지기는 각 장소에 있는 뮤온의 양을 측정하는 데 쓰입니다. 입자가 상대적으로 많을 때 탐지기는 빈 공간을 어두운 색으로 알려줍니다.

그러면, 우리는 그 장소의 대략적인 그림과 내부 구조를 짐작할 수 있습니다. 어떻게 CT가 X레이를 이용해 몸의 입체구조를 나타내는지를 알고 있다면 그것은 이해하기 그리 어렵지 않습니다. 의학적인 개념으로 보면, 이것은 단층촬영과 매우 유사한 개념입니다. 이제, 뮤온탐지기와 함께, 우리는 그 장소를 파보기 전에 그 안에 무엇이 있는지 볼 수 있죠. 이것은 우리가 필요한 부분만 발굴함으로써 손상을 최소화해주기 때문에 실용적입니다. 매우 작은 손상도 중요한 정보를 영원히 잃을 수 있게 한다는 점에서 고고학자들은 매우 조심해야 합니다.

Still, muon detectors weren't always this convenient. Muon detectors were proven to work in 1967 when a physicist buried these detectors in the ground surrounding the Colosseum. Although his search for buried chambers failed to yield any surprises, it showed the advantage of the technique, as well as its need for improvement. For one, the size of the machine he used was so big that it was comparable to that of a water heater. This hampered the machine's mobility and made many archeologists doubt its practicality. In addition, the range seemed unsatisfactory because the detector in 1967 could only scan muons above it, which means that it couldn't observe structures in the left or right. Meaning the machine had to be placed beneath the Colosseum in order to view the inner structure of the historical relic. Another issue was time, since it took a year for the 1967 study to get the results.

As the muon detector continues to improve, I believe we'll see muons being applied in various ways. It won't be too long before muon detectors are utilized in other areas of science. In my opinion, there's a possibility that they may prove useful for scoping our nuclear waste sites or even looking underground.

하지만, 뮤온탐지기가 늘 이렇게 편리했던 것은 아닙니다. 뮤온탐지기는 1967년 한 물리학자가 이 탐지기들을 콜로세움 근처에 묻었을 때 작동하는 것이 증명되었습니다. 비록 숨겨진 방들을 찾기 위한 그의 노력은 놀라운 결과를 산출해내지 못했지만, 그것은 그 기술의 장점과 앞으로 발전이 필요한 부분을 알게 해주었습니다. 첫 번째로 그가 사용했던 기계의 크기가 너무 커서, 온탕기와 비견할 만했습니다. 이것은 이 기계의 이동성을 심각하게 저해시켜서 많은 고고학자들이 실용성을 의심했죠. 또한, 1967년의 탐지기는 그 위에 있는 뮤온들만 스캔할 수 있었기 때문에 그 범위 또한 만족스럽지 못하였습니다. 이것은 왼쪽이나 오른쪽에 있는 구조물을 관측하지 못한다는 것을 의미합니다. 즉, 역사적 유물들의 내부 구조를 보기 위해 기계는 콜로세움 아래에 놓여야 했습니다. 또 다른 문제는 시간이었습니다. 1967년의 연구의 결과를 얻기까지 일 년이 걸렸기 때문이죠.

뮤온탐지기가 계속해서 발전하기 때문에, 저는 우리가 앞으로 더 다양한 곳에 뮤온이 적용되는 것을 볼 수 있을 거라 생각합니다. 뮤온탐지기가 과학의 다른 분야에 쓰이는 데까지 걸리는 시간은 그렇게 길지 않을 것입니다. 제 생각엔, 핵 폐기장 관찰에도 쓰일 수 있을 것이고 또는 지하를 탐험하는 데에도 쓰일 가능성이 있습니다.

어휘_ array 집합체 muon 경입자족 중 하나로 π중간자 및 K중간자가 붕괴할 때 생기는 불안정한 입자 detector 탐지기 elementary particle 소립자(물질을 이루는 가장 작은 단위의 물질을 소립자라고 한다.) electron 전자 cosmic ray 우주선 proton 양성자 molecule 분자 disintegrate 해체되다, 산산조각 나다 intrigue 강한 흥미를 불러일으키다 penetrate 뚫고 들어가다; 관통하다 꿰뚫어 보다 tomography 단층촬영; 몸의 한 단면만을 촬영하는 X선 검사법 practicality 실용성 scoping (평가 · 감상을 위한) 살펴보기, 관찰, 검사 nuclear waste site 핵 폐기장

---

6. **What does the professor mainly discuss?**
   - ⓐ Widely accepted myths concerning the study of archaeology
   - ⓑ A historical site that was excavated with the aid of a muon detector
   - ⓒ The combination of physics and archaeology to develop a technology
   - ⓓ Positive aspects of muon detectors for archaeologists

교수는 주로 무엇에 관해서 이야기하는가?
   - ⓐ 고고학과 관련된 널리 알려진 근거 없는 믿음
   - ⓑ 뮤온탐지기의 도움으로 발굴된 역사적 장소
   - ⓒ 한 기술을 발전시키기 위한 물리학과 고고학의 결합
   - ⓓ 고고학자들에게 뮤온탐지기가 가지는 긍정적인 측면

7. According to the professor, why are muon used in archaeology?

  Ⓐ Because they can carry and transmit electrical charges

  Ⓑ Because they degrade cosmic rays into more basic components

  Ⓒ Because they travel through solid material

  Ⓓ Because they can produce 3-D pictures

교수의 말에 따르면, 뮤온은 왜 고고학 분야에서 쓰이는가?

  Ⓐ 그것들이 전하를 운송하고 전달하기 때문에

  Ⓑ 그것들이 우주선을 더 기본적 원소들로 저하시키기 때문에

  Ⓒ 그것들이 단단한 물질을 통과하기 때문에

  Ⓓ 그것들이 입체적인 사진들을 생산할 수 있기 때문에

8. What can a muon detector reveal about the colosseum?

  Ⓐ The darkness of the inner region

  Ⓑ The structure of underground rooms

  Ⓒ The strength of its foundation

  Ⓓ The material composing the walls

뮤온탐지기가 콜로세움에 대해서 알려주는 것은 무엇인가?

  Ⓐ 안쪽 지역의 어두운 부분

  Ⓑ 지하에 있는 방들의 구조

  Ⓒ 건물 토대의 탄탄함

  Ⓓ 벽들을 구성하고 있는 물질들

9. Why does the professor mention CT scans?

  Ⓐ To discuss the possibility of using muon detectors in medicine

  Ⓑ To compare archaeological diagrams with medical ones

  Ⓒ To emphasize the role of technology in scientific fields

  Ⓓ To explain the imaging process of muon detectors

왜 교수는 CT스캔을 언급하는가?

  Ⓐ 뮤온탐지기를 의료 분야에 사용할 수 있는 가능성을 말하기 위해

  Ⓑ 고고학적 도표와 의학적 도표를 비교하기 위해

  Ⓒ 과학 분야에서 기술의 역할을 강조하기 위해

  Ⓓ 뮤온탐지기의 이미지 생성 과정을 설명하기 위해

10. Why were muon detectors unpopular in 1967? **Click on 3 answers.**

  Ⓐ They were expensive to build.

  Ⓑ They required an energy source.

  Ⓒ They were too large.

  Ⓓ They were slow to produce an image.

  Ⓔ They were inconvenient depending on a certain condition.

1967년에는 왜 뮤온탐지기가 인기가 없었는가? **정답을 3개 클릭하시오.**

  Ⓐ 그것들은 만들기 비쌌다.

  Ⓑ 그것들은 에너지원을 요구했다.

  Ⓒ 그것들은 너무 컸다.

  Ⓓ 그것들은 이미지를 생성하는 데 시간이 걸렸다.

  Ⓔ 그것들은 특정한 조건일 때 불편했다.

11. What does the professor imply about newer muon detectors?

  Ⓐ They can be used to develop clean energy.

  Ⓑ They will gain popularity among archaeologists.

  Ⓒ They have potential in several scientific fields.

  Ⓓ They are more accurate than older detectors.

새로운 뮤온탐지기에 대해 교수는 무엇을 암시하는가?

  Ⓐ 그들은 깨끗한 자원을 발전시키는 데 쓰일 수 있다.

  Ⓑ 그들은 고고학자들 사이에서 인기를 얻을 것이다.

  Ⓒ 그들은 여러 과학적 분야에 잠재적 발전 가능성을 가지고 있다.

  Ⓓ 그들은 이전의 탐지기들보다 더 정확하다.

12. Ⓑ	13. Ⓑ	14. Ⓑ	15. Ⓐ	16. Ⓑ	17. Ⓒ

[Questions 12-17] Listen to part of a lecture in a paleontology class.
고생물학 수업의 강의 일부분을 들으시오.

Test2_Listening_Part1_12-17.mp3

P Last time we covered the topic of dinosaur fossils of the Mesozoic era, that ended approximately 65 million years ago. Today, we will cover the sauropods. These dinosaurs were the biggest herbivores in existence and were usually quite long-necked quadrupeds. Of course, there are some interesting speculations about these animals, but I'd rather focus on how these gigantic animals could flourish on the Earth. As I've explained in the last class, we have learned through fossils that sauropods were one of the largest animals to walk on the Earth! In fact, their size was even greater than that of the blue whale, the largest living animal of today. Sauropods weighed up to one hundred tons, that's more than twenty elephants. Just think about that, twenty elephants!! Furthermore, the sauropods survived for a great length of time. There are fossil records of sauropods that span over one hundred million years.

S How and why were these sauropods able to successfully flourish on the Earth? Wouldn't it be difficult for such a huge animal to survive since they're relatively recessive?

P You are right. In a biological sense, it is hard to understand how such huge animals were successful at survival. For example, large animals like elephants require a tremendous amount of energy and food consumption to account for their sizes. This makes it hard to maintain a stable population level and this is why the largest animals today live in the ocean, where they can easily access large quantities of food and

P 지난 시간에, 우리는 약 6천 5백만 년 전에 끝난 중생대의 공룡화석에 대한 주제를 다뤘습니다. 오늘 우리는 용각류 공룡에 대해 배우겠습니다. 이러한 공룡들은 가장 큰 초식동물이며 긴 목을 가진 네발짐승이었습니다. 물론 이 동물에 대해 많은 흥미로운 추측들이 있지만 저는 이 거대한 동물이 어떻게 이 땅에서 번성할 수 있었는지에 초점을 맞출까 합니다. 지난 시간에 설명했듯이, 화석을 보았을 때 용각류 공룡은 지구상에 걸어다니는 가장 큰 동물 중 하나였습니다. 사실 그 크기는 오늘날 지구에 살아 있는 동물 중 가장 큰 흰긴수염고래보다 훨씬 큽니다. 용각류 공룡은 무게가 100톤이 넘었는데 이는 코끼리 20마리보다도 무거운 것입니다. 무려 20마리요! 게다가, 이 공룡은 오랫동안 생존했습니다. 이 공룡이 1억 년이 넘게 살았다는 화석 증거들이 있습니다.

S 어떻게 이 공룡이 성공적으로 지구에서 번성할 수 있었나요? 큰 동물들은 상대적으로 열성이기 때문에 살기 힘들지 않나요?

P 맞아요. 생물학적인 관점에서 이런 용각류 공룡들이 어떻게 번성했는지 이해하는 것은 힘듭니다. 예를 들어 코끼리 같은 큰 동물들은 크기에 걸맞은 많은 양의 에너지와 소비를 필요로 합니다. 이는 안정적인 개체 수 유지를 힘들게 하기 때문에 오늘날 거대 동물들이 많은 먹이를 접근하기 편한 바다에 삽니다. 예를 들어 흰긴수염고래는 매일 8,000파운드의 먹이를 먹습니다. 게다가 거대 동물들은 과열된 체온을 낮추는 게

maintain their body temperature. For example, blue whales consume 8,000 pounds of food per day. Moreover, it is very difficult for large animals to get rid of excessive body heat. Obviously, blue whales in the ocean don't have a problem with that, since the temperature of the ocean is relatively cool. On the other hand, 100-ton sauropods would be much more affected by this body heat issue. Generally, even the most ardent advocates of warm-blooded dinosaurs back off when it comes to sauropods, since simulations show that these oversized animals would have baked themselves from the inside, like a potato, if they generated too much internal metabolic energy. So, today, the prevalence of opinion is that sauropods were cold-blooded, which is, they managed to maintain a near-constant body temperature because they warmed up and cooled off depending their environment.

Another problem concerns the procurement of large amounts of food. For a long time, scientists believed that it was the vast plantations of the Mesozoic era that allowed the sauropods to thrive. However, after it had been discovered that there were much lower oxygen levels during the Mesozoic era, they concluded that there was much less plant life available for the sauropods to consume.

Therefore, to now figure out the survival techniques of the sauropods, the scientists are analyzing these giants by comparing the differences of the sauropod fossils and the anatomy of today's animals. The most reliable source of evidence was that the sauropods were very effective energy conservers. Their stomachs had an enormous capacity for the digestion of food over a long period of time, allowing then to store energy and use it in a slow and gradual manner for situations where they really needed it. With the help of a large stomach and slow digestion, the sauropods were able to spend

힘듭니다. 당연히 흰긴수염고래는 그런 문제점을 가지고 있지 않습니다. 왜냐하면 바다의 온도는 상대적으로 낮기 때문이지요. 반면에 100톤의 공룡은 매우 어려웠을 것입니다. 일반적으로 공룡이 온혈동물이라고 주장하는 대부분의 사람들조차도 용각류 공룡들에 대해서라면 뒤로 물러납니다. 왜냐하면 만약 그들이 내부에서 너무 많은 신진 에너지를 만들어내면, 이러한 거대 동물들은 감자처럼 안에서부터 익어버린다는 것을 시뮬레이션이 보여줬기 때문이지요. 그래서 오늘날 대다수 사람들은 용각류 공룡들을 환경에 따라 체온이 오르고 식기 때문에 가까스로 체온을 유지하는 냉혈동물이라고 생각합니다.

또 다른 문제점은 음식의 조달입니다. 오랜 시간 동안, 과학자들은 중생대의 많은 식물들이 이 용각류 공룡들을 번성하게 해주었다고 생각했습니다. 하지만, 중생대 동안 산소의 양이 훨씬 적었음이 발견된 후, 이 공룡이 섭취할 식물이 훨씬 적었다고 결론 내렸습니다.

그러므로, 현재 과학자들은 이 용각류 공룡들의 생존 기술을 알아내기 위해, 오늘날 동물의 해부 구조와 공룡 화석의 차이점을 비교하면서 이 거대 동물을 분석하고 있습니다. 가장 믿을 수 있는 증거는 이 용각류 공룡들은 에너지 보존이 매우 효율적이라는 것입니다. 그들의 위는 오랜 시간 동안 음식을 소화시킬 수 있는 거대한 용량을 가지고 있어, 에너지를 저장하고 필요한 상황에서 그 에너지를 천천히 사용할 수 있습니다. 이 큰 위와 느린 소화 덕분에 이 공룡은 에너지와 음식을 찾는 시간을 줄일 수 있었습니다. 우리는 어떻게 용각류 공룡들이 오랜 기간 느리게 소화함으로써 신진대사를 늦추는 능력을 개발하면서 환경

less energy and time constantly trying to find food. We could see how sauropods adapted to this environment by developing the ability to slow their metabolism down by digesting slowly for extended periods. As a result, this is why sauropods could maintain a high survival rate even with little food. I guess this is a feature that most people would envy.

Another interesting theory is that sauropods could not chew food. The sauropod's skull structure did not show any evidence of chewing muscles. This would be similar to modern day birds and reptiles, the kind of animals that also can't chew. Because they can't chew their food, these animals have other special ways for digesting their food. Some of them even swallow stones called gastroliths that grind up the food in the stomach. Interestingly, sauropod fossils are frequently found alongside these smooth stones. The scientists have assumed that these were gastroliths. However, by comparing the smooth stones with current day organisms' stones it has been concluded that the stone discovered with the saurpod fossils was not gastrolith.

By comparing this fossil evidence with the biology of today's animals, scientists were able to learn that sauropods in fact did not eat gastroliths to help their digestion. For example, study shows that ostriches have to consume gastroliths that amount up to one percent of the body weight. However, the smooth stones discovered with the sauropod was too light in its proportion. Thus, other researchers hypothesized that sauropods could have consumed these stones as their source of mineral such as calcium. A theory proposes that they might have ingested the stones as a substitute when not enough food sources were available, in order to survive.

에 적응해왔는지 이해할 수 있습니다. 이것이 용각류 공룡들이 극히 적은 음식으로도 높은 생존율을 유지할 수 있는 이유예요. 저는 이것이 대부분의 사람들이 부러워하는 모습이라고 생각합니다.

또 다른 흥미로운 이론은 이 용각류 공룡들이 음식을 씹지 못했을 수도 있다는 것입니다. 공룡의 두개골 구조를 보면 씹는 근육이 보이지 않습니다. 이것은 현재 새나 파충류와 비슷합니다. 이런 종류의 동물은 씹지 못하지요. 그들은 음식을 씹지 못하기 때문에 음식을 소화시키는 다른 방법을 가지고 있습니다. 그들 중 일부는 심지어 위에서 음식물을 갈아주는 위결석이라 불리는 돌을 삼키기도 합니다. 흥미롭게도 이 공룡의 화석은 부드러운 돌들 옆에서 종종 발견되었습니다. 과학자들은 이것들이 위결석이라고 가정해왔습니다. 하지만 오늘날 유기체의 돌들과 이 부드러운 돌을 비교할 때, 공룡 화석과 함께 발견된 돌은 위결석이 아니라고 결론지어졌습니다.

오늘날 동물과 이 화석 증거를 비교하면서 과학자들은 이 공룡들이 소화를 돕기 위해서 위결석을 섭취하지 않았다는 사실을 배울 수 있었습니다. 예를 들어 연구는 타조가 몸무게의 1퍼센트의 위결석을 섭취해야 한다고 보여줬습니다. 하지만 공룡 뼈 옆에서 발견된 부드러운 돌들은 비율상으로 너무 가벼웠습니다. 그러므로 다른 연구자들은 이 공룡이 칼슘 같은 미네랄 원료로 이 돌들을 섭취했을 수도 있다는 가설을 세웠습니다. 이 이론은 공룡들이 아마도 음식이 충분하지 않을 때 대체물로 돌들을 섭취했을 거라고 제안합니다.

어휘_ sauropods 용각류 (초식) 공룡 blue whale 흰긴수염고래 procurement 조달 gastroliths 위결석 hypothesize 가설을 세우다 substitute 대체물

12. What is the lecture mainly about?

Ⓐ Describing the digestion mechanics of the sauropods

Ⓑ Discussing the proposals about the adaptation of recessive animals

Ⓒ Illustrating the difficulties faced by the sauropods while evolving

Ⓓ Comparing the differences of sauropods and ocean blue whales

강의는 주로 무엇에 관한 것인가?

Ⓐ 용각류 공룡들의 소화 구조를 묘사하는 것

Ⓑ 열성 동물들의 적응에 대한 제안들을 논의하는 것

Ⓒ 진화하는 동안 용각류 공룡들이 직면한 어려움들을 설명하는 것

Ⓓ 용각류 공룡들과 바다의 흰긴수염고래의 차이점들을 비교하는 것

13. Why does the professor mention the blue whales?

Ⓐ To introduce a contemporary counterpart of sauropods that live in the oceans

Ⓑ To emphasize the size and biological features of sauropods

Ⓒ To illustrate how big the blue whales are compared to sauropods

Ⓓ To emphasize the impressive size of blue whales

교수는 왜 흰긴수염고래를 언급하는가?

Ⓐ 바다에 사는 용각류 공룡과 현재 동일한 동물을 소개하기 위해서

Ⓑ 용각류 공룡들의 크기와 생물학적 특징을 강조하기 위해서

Ⓒ 용각류 공룡들과 비교해서 흰긴수염고래가 얼마나 큰지 설명하기 위해서

Ⓓ 흰긴수염고래의 인상적인 크기를 강조하기 위해서

Listen again to a part of the conversation. Then answer the question.
대화의 일부분을 듣고 질문에 답하시오.

Sauropods weighed up to one hundred tons, that's more than twenty elephants. Just think about that, twenty elephants!!

용각류 공룡은 무게가 100톤이 넘었는데 이는 코끼리 20마리보다도 무거운 것입니다. 무려 20마리요!

14. Why does the professor say this: 🎧 It's twenty elephants!!

Ⓐ She wants the students to challenge this assertion.

Ⓑ She thinks this number is very impressive.

Ⓒ She does not think this information is reliable.

Ⓓ She thinks this information is particularly important.

교수가 왜 이것을 말하는가?: 무려 20마리요!

Ⓐ 그녀는 학생들이 이 주장에 이의를 제기하기를 원한다.

Ⓑ 그녀는 이 숫자가 대단히 인상적이라고 생각한다.

Ⓒ 그녀는 이 정보가 믿을 수 없다고 생각한다.

Ⓓ 그녀는 이 정보가 특히 중요하다고 생각한다.

15. **Why does the professor mention potatoes?**
   Ⓐ To support that sauropods could not have controlled their temperature internally
   Ⓑ To imply that sauropods struggled to regulate their temperature because the Earth was too hot
   Ⓒ To emphasize that many warm-blooded animals have thrived on the Earth
   Ⓓ To illustrate that sauropods are too big to be compared to potatoes

왜 교수는 감자들을 언급하는가?
   Ⓐ 용각류 공룡들이 내부적으로 체온을 조절할 수 없었을 것임을 지지하기 위해서
   Ⓑ 용각류 공룡들이 지구가 너무 뜨거웠기 때문에 그들의 온도를 조절하는 게 힘들었다는 것을 암시하기 위해서
   Ⓒ 지구에 많은 온혈동물들이 번성했다는 것을 강조하기 위해서
   Ⓓ 용각류 공룡들이 감자들과 비교해서 너무 크다는 것을 설명하기 위해서

16. **According to the professor, how did sauropods manage with a shortage of food?**
   Ⓐ Plantations provided a variety of plants as food.
   Ⓑ Slow digestion allowed the efficient use of energy.
   Ⓒ Food that did not require chewing was plentiful.
   Ⓓ Gastroliths supplied necessary minerals.

교수에 따르면, 용각류 공룡들은 어떻게 음식 부족에서 살아남을 수 있었는가?
   Ⓐ 목초지에서 음식으로 다양한 종류의 식물들을 제공했다.
   Ⓑ 느린 소화가 효과적인 에너지 사용을 도왔다.
   Ⓒ 씹을 필요가 없는 음식이 풍부했다.
   Ⓓ 위결석이 충분한 미네랄을 제공했다.

Listen again to a part of the conversation. Then answer the question.
대화의 일부분을 듣고 질문에 답하시오.

As a result, this is why sauropods could maintain a high survival rate even with little food. I guess this is a feature that most people would envy.

이것이 용각류 공룡들이 극히 적은 음식으로도 높은 생존율을 유지할 수 있는 이유예요. 저는 이것이 대부분의 사람들이 부러워하는 모습이라고 생각해요.

17. **What does the professor mean when she says this: 🎧 I guess this is a feature that most people would envy.**
   Ⓐ People should learn about sauropods' digestive pattern.
   Ⓑ People should conduct more research on the behavior of sauropods.
   Ⓒ Sauropods' way of adaptation is extremely efficient.
   Ⓓ Sauropods are more intelligent than human beings in some ways.

교수는 이것을 말할 때 무엇을 의미하는가?: 저는 이것이 대부분의 사람들이 부러워하는 모습이라고 생각해요.
   Ⓐ 사람들은 용각류 공룡들의 소화 패턴을 배우는 것이 좋다.
   Ⓑ 사람들은 용각류 공룡들의 행동에 대한 더 많은 연구를 하는 것이 좋다.
   Ⓒ 용각류 공룡들의 적응 방법은 굉장히 효율적이다.
   Ⓓ 용각류 공룡들은 몇 가지 방법에서 사람보다 더 지능적이다.

1. Ⓓ   **2.** Ⓓ   **3.** Ⓒ   **4.** Ⓐ   **5.** Ⓒ

[Questions 1-5] Listen to part of a conversation between a student and a professor.
학생과 교수님의 대화 일부분을 들으시오.

Test2_Listening_Part2_01-05.mp3

S Dr. Ramiro? Sorry I'm a little late.	S 라미로 박사님? 조금 늦어서 죄송해요.
P It's fine. It actually gave me time to review your research proposal.	P 괜찮아. 사실, 너의 연구 계획서를 검토할 시간이 되었거든.
S Oh, that's a relief. So, um, what did you think?	S 오, 다행이네요. 그럼, 음, 어떻게 생각하세요?
P Well, it's reasonably well-presented but if you're serious about getting that grant then you might want to make a few improvements. For one, you should explain how you're planning to get a more focused statistical analysis.	P 음, 상당히 잘 되어 있어. 하지만 만약 보조금 받는 것을 중요하게 생각한다면, 몇몇 부분을 개선하는 게 좋을 거야. 하나를 들자면, 어떻게 더 집중된 통계적 분석을 얻어낼 계획인지를 설명해야 해.
S Yeah, you're probably right. I just… I don't know how to get that done.	S 네. 교수님 말씀이 아마 맞을 거예요. 저는… 그것을 어떻게 하는지를 모르겠어요.
P Hmm. Did you try going to the Computer Center? The woman at the information desk… Jess, I think, can help you find a statistician. That should be someone who can teach you how to set up your experiment in order to get your statistics in a meaningful form. After you get that part done, you'll need to explain the procedure in your proposal.	P 음, 컴퓨터 센터에 가본 적이 있니? 안내 데스크에 여자가 있는데, 내가 알기로는 제스일 거야. 그녀가 통계 전문가를 찾는 것을 도와줄 수 있어. 그 사람이 너의 통계수치들을 의미 있는 형태로 얻기 위해 어떻게 실험해야 하는지를 알려줄 거야. 그 부분이 끝나고 나면 제안서에 있는 절차를 설명해야 해.
S I never thought of the Computer Center.	S 컴퓨터 센터 같은 것은 전혀 생각해보지 않았어요.
P It's a good thing I told you, then. Also, remember to submit your proposal before the office closes on Friday and make sure you have a clear idea of how you aim to deal with your data.	P 내가 알려줘서 잘됐구나. 그리고 금요일에 사무실 문을 닫기 전에 제안서를 제출해야 한다는 것을 명심하렴. 너의 자료들을 다루는 목적을 확실히 해.
S Okay, I definitely won't miss the deadline. So, should I get going?	S 알겠어요. 마감기한은 반드시 지킬게요. 그럼 이대로 시작하는 게 좋을까요?
P Not yet. Your proposal needs more than one improvement. Here, take a look at the proposal you gave me. I wrote some comments… like this one. I'm concerned about the lack of	P 아니, 아직. 너의 제안서는 여러 군데 손볼 필요가 있어. 여기, 네가 나에게 준 제안서를 봐봐, 이 부분같이 몇 가지 코멘트를 달아놓았어. 실험 대상들에 대한 정의가 부족한 것

definition of your subjects. I understand that you want to test how non-native speakers understand English stress patterns, correct? But who exactly are these subjects that will be tested on the subtle differences in English pronunciation? It seems to me that you haven't clearly defined the group of subjects in your proposal.

S I've rounded up a group of international students to work on the project with me. Uh, I told you that, didn't I?

P Yes but it has to be in your proposal. You see, there are some issues that the committee will question. Your proposal right now is… to put it simply, you're comparing apples and oranges. We've talked about your subjects being given an oral fluency test so that you can choose subjects with a similar linguistics level. When you put that down on your proposal, the committee will say… well, The committee will say that comparing English stress patterns between a German native speaker and a Japanese native speaker is meaningless. Because German, like English, has its roots in Latin, it will resemble English. Thus, the two cannot be compared. Do you see how your data has a potential of becoming ambiguous? You need to be very clear about how you're going to select your subjects.

S Would it help if I write more about the oral test we talked about?

P Of course. There's a good start.

S Thanks for pointing all that out. I never would have realized all that … oh, um, Dr. Ramiro, I have class in about 20 minutes. I'm going to drop by the Computer Center, since it's on my way to the classroom building. Could we continue this talk at around 3:30?

P Sorry, Diane, I can't. How about you take this proposal back, read my comments, and work

이 염려가 되는구나. 난 영어가 모국어가 아닌 사람들이 어떻게 영어의 강세 패턴들을 이해하는지에 대해 실험하기를 원한다고 이해했는데, 맞니? 그런데 이 미묘한 영어 발음의 차이점을 실험할 수 있는 이 실험 대상자들이 정확하게 누구야? 내가 보기에는 네가 제안서에 실험 대상자 그룹을 명백하게 정의하지 않은 거 같아.

S 저는 저와 함께 이 프로젝트를 할 유학생들을 모았어요. 어, 제가 말씀드리지 않았었나요?

P 맞아. 하지만 제안서에 그 부분에 대한 설명이 있어야만 해. 알다시피 위원회에서 궁금증을 가질 만한 몇 가지 논쟁거리가 있거든. 너의 제안서는… 예를 들자면, 전혀 다른 두 가지를 비교하고 있어. 네가 실험 대상자들에게 언어의 유창성을 말로 테스트할 거라고 했고, 그래서 비슷한 언어 수준의 대상자들을 선택할 거라고 했어. 그런데 네가 그것을 제안서에 써 넣으면 독어가 모국어인 사람과 일어가 모국어인 사람의 영어 강세 패턴을 비교하는 것이 무슨 의미가 있냐고 위원회에서 말할 거야. 당연히 영어처럼 독어도 라틴어 어원이기 때문에 영어와 닮았을 거야. 이 두 개를 비교할 수는 없지. 네 자료가 어떻게 모호해질 가능성이 생겼는지 이해했니? 너는 어떻게 실험 대상자를 선택했는지에 대해 매우 분명해야 해.

S 만일 제가 저희가 논의한 구두시험에 대한 것을 더 쓴다면 괜찮아질까요?

P 물론이지. 시작이 좋구나.

S 모든 것을 지적해주셔서 감사해요. 저는 결코 생각지도 못했던 것들이에요. 라미로 박사님, 제가 20분 후에 수업이 있는데, 가는 길에 컴퓨터 센터에 들르려고 하거든요. 수업 들으러 가는 길에 있어서요. 3시 30분쯤에 이야기를 다시 할 수 있을까요?

P 미안해, 다이앤. 우선 이 제안서를 가져가서, 내가 언급한 부분들을 읽고 실험에 대한 선

on your subject selection? I'll read your next draft if you can turn it in by tomorrow morning. Then we can work out the final details and you'll have time to make changes before finally turning it in.

S That sounds great. Thanks for all your help, Dr. Ramiro!

택을 해보는 건 어떨까? 내일 아침까지 네가 제출할 수 있다면 다음 초고를 읽겠어. 그다음에 세부적인 내용들을 논의하면 네가 마지막으로 제출하기 전까지 수정할 시간이 있을 거야.

S 좋아요, 라미로 박사님. 도와주셔서 감사합니다.

어휘_ non-native 모국어 사용자가 아닌 subtle 미묘한 committee 위원회 apples and oranges 전혀 다른 두 가지

---

1. What is the conversation about?
Ⓐ The problems about defining test subjects
Ⓑ The submission of a proposal by Friday
Ⓒ The student's problem with analyzing statistics
Ⓓ The need for improvements in the proposal

대화는 무엇에 관한 것인가?
Ⓐ 실험 대상을 정의하는 것에 대한 문제점들
Ⓑ 금요일까지 제안서의 제출
Ⓒ 통계자료들을 분석하는 데 학생의 문제점
Ⓓ 제안서에서 개선해야 할 것

2. Why does the professor mention the computer center?
Ⓐ The student should search the Web for statistical information.
Ⓑ The student could receive specific advice about choosing test subjects.
Ⓒ The student can find Jess who is a helpful woman at the information desk.
Ⓓ The student may get some help setting up the statistical analysis.

교수는 왜 컴퓨터 센터를 언급하는가?
Ⓐ 학생이 통계 정보들을 인터넷으로 찾아보아야 한다.
Ⓑ 실험 대상을 선택하는 것에 있어서 구체적인 조언을 들을 수 있다.
Ⓒ 학생이 인포메이션 데스크에서 도움을 받을 수 있는 여자인 제스를 찾을 수 있다.
Ⓓ 학생은 정보적인 분석을 만들어내기 위한 도움을 얻을 수 있다.

3. According to the professor, how should the student modify her proposal?
Ⓐ She should outline the process of choosing her statistical analysis.
Ⓑ She should explain the meaning of her statistics to the committee.
Ⓒ She should explain more about the selection of her subjects.
Ⓓ She should add personal information about the international students.

교수에 따르면, 학생은 그녀의 제안서를 어떻게 수정해야 하는가?
Ⓐ 그녀는 통계 분석을 선택하는 과정을 서술해야 한다.
Ⓑ 그녀는 통계자료들의 의미를 위원회에 설명하는 것이 좋다.
Ⓒ 그녀는 실험 대상들의 선택에 대해 더 설명해야 한다.
Ⓓ 그녀는 유학생들에 대한 개인적인 정보를 추가해야 한다.

Yes, but it has to be in your proposal. You see, there are some issues that the committee will question. Your proposal right now is… to give you an example, you're comparing apples and oranges.

맞아. 하지만 제안서에 그 부분에 대한 설명이 있어야만 해. 알다시피 위원회에서 궁금증을 가질 만한 몇 가지 논쟁거리가 있거든. 너의 제안서는… 예를 들자면, 전혀 다른 두 가지를 비교하고 있어. 네가 실험 대상자들에게 언어의 유창성을 말로 테스트할 거라고 했고, 그래서 비슷한 언어 수준의 대상자들을 선택할 거라고 했어.

4. What does the professor imply when he says this:
🎧 Your proposal right now is… to give you an example, you're comparing apples and oranges.
Ⓐ To indicate a shortcoming in the student's proposal
Ⓑ To contrast two different kinds of language speakers
Ⓒ To illustrate the dissimilar linguistic levels of international students
Ⓓ To emphasize the variety of subjects for the student's research

왜 교수는 이것을 말하는가?: 너의 제안서는… 예를 들자면, 전혀 다른 두 가지를 비교하고 있어.
Ⓐ 학생의 제안서의 단점을 설명하기 위해서
Ⓑ 두 가지 다른 종류의 언어 사용자를 대조하기 위해서
Ⓒ 유학생들의 다른 언어의 정도를 설명하기 위해서
Ⓓ 학생의 연구를 위한 다양한 실험 대상들을 강조하기 위해서

5. What does the professor imply about the people in the committee?
Ⓐ They will expect her to go to the Computer Center.
Ⓑ They probably don't understand the stress patterns she is researching.
Ⓒ They will question her process of comparing test subjects.
Ⓓ They will be particularly selective and discriminating toward her.

교수는 위원회에 있는 사람들에 대해 무엇을 암시하는가?
Ⓐ 그들은 컴퓨터 센터에 학생이 가기를 기대할 것이다.
Ⓑ 그들은 아마도 학생이 연구하는 강세 패턴을 이해하지 못할 것이다.
Ⓒ 그들은 실험 대상자들을 비교하는 과정에 대해 질문할 것이다.
Ⓓ 그들은 그녀에게 특히 까다롭고 그녀를 차별할 것이다.

Part 2　Questions 6-11

6. Ⓑ　　　**7.** Ⓓ　　　**8.** Ⓐ　　　**9.** Ⓓ, Ⓔ　　　**10.** Ⓓ　　　**11.** Ⓒ

[Questions 6-11] Listen to part of a lecture in a geology class.
지질학 강의 일부분을 들으시오.

Test2_Listening_Part2_06-11.mp3

Visually speaking, the Earth might seem static but in reality, it is not. the Earth surface constantly changes by continually working natural forces. A lot of these changes happen so gradually that it is very hard to witness the progress; of course, that doesn't mean the Earth shift is not happening. The Earth has been undergoing these gradual shifts for thousands of years. This is a basic type of geological science called uniformitarianism.

Uniformitarianism advocates that various geological forces such as erosion and uplifts shaped today's the Earth as well as the Earth in the past. Furthermore, uniformitarianism states that these forces are consistently modifying the Earth's shape slowly at a similarly speedy and gradual intensity. This ideology could also be applied to analyze the details of the Earth's past by observing the changes on the Earth occurring today.

To rewind our conversation for a moment, uniformitarianism is one of the most basic guidelines of geology that has been developed over 200 years. Given its solid foundation, how would you feel if someone challenged this long-standing theory? One scientist asserted that the feature of the Earth's surface has changed not by slow gradual shifts but it actually evolved by a single abrupt catastrophic event carried by an extreme intensity. This hypothesis was greatly ridiculed by a lot of scientists who believed in the well-established uniformitarianism. As a result, not a whole lot of geologists wanted to review the evidence on this scientist's hypothesis.

시각적으로 말하자면, 지구는 정적인 것처럼 보일 수 있지만, 실제로는 그렇지 않습니다. 지구 표면은 끊임없이 지속적으로 작용하는 자연적인 힘에 의해 변경됩니다. 이러한 많은 변화들은 너무 점진적으로 일어나서 진보를 목격하기는 매우 힘듭니다. 당연히 이것이 지구의 움직임이 일어나지 않는다는 것은 아니지요. 지구는 수천 년 전부터 이러한 점진적 이동을 진행해왔습니다. 이것이 동일과정설이라고 불리는 지질 과학의 기본 유형입니다.

동일과정설은 오늘날의 지구와 과거의 지구를 형성한 침식 및 융기 등과 같은 다양한 지질학적인 힘을 지지합니다. 또한, 동일과정설은 이러한 힘들이 지속적으로 지구의 모양을 비슷한 속도와 점진적인 강도로 느리게 변화시키고 있다는 것을 설명합니다. 이 개념은 또한 오늘날 지구에 발생하는 변화를 관찰함으로써 지구의 과거에 대해 세부적으로 분석하는 일에 적용될 수 있습니다.

우리의 강의를 잠시 떠올려보면, 동일과정설은 200년 이상 발전해온 지질학의 가장 기본적인 지침 중의 하나입니다. 그것의 튼튼한 기초를 감안할 때, 당신은 누군가가 이 오래된 이론에 도전한다면 어떻게 느끼시겠습니까? 한 과학자가 지구 표면의 특징은 서서히 점차적으로 움직여서가 아니라 사실은 갑작스러운 엄청난 세기의 재해에 의해 변한 것이라고 주장했습니다. 이 가설은 잘 확립된 동일과정설을 믿는 많은 과학자들에게 매우 비웃음당했습니다. 그래서 많은 지질학자들이 이 과학자의 가설에 대한 증거를 훑어보기를 원하지도 않았습니다.

However, there was a scientist, named James Harlen Bretz, who had turned in his analysis of this interesting hypothesis to the professional conference of geologists. In his paper, Bretz elaborated on the details of the formation of a unique landscape called channeled scablands which formed the current day State of Washington in the northwestern part of the United States.

These scablands are considered unique because these areas contained lots of gigantic canyons and massive waterfalls. It has been noted that such landscapes do not exist anywhere in the entire world and geologists have failed to produce an adequate explanation for how it was formed. Bretz explained that a huge flood, a catastrophic geological event that had happened in a single night, had shaped this landscape during the ice age. Other types of hypothesis came up as well, that mostly shared the view of the uniformitarianists; these geologists explained that gradual repeated forces applied a cumulative power that would amount up to the force of a sudden huge change.

However, constant research concluded that the scablands yielded no evidence of changes occurring over time. In turn, as most geologists had strongly believed in the uniformitarianism, they neglected such theories that went against their beliefs. They justified themselves, believing that by doing so they were saving not only geology but also other types of sciences as well, along with considering that even Charles Darwin's theory of natural selection had much influence on uniformitarianism. Darwin argued most organisms changed and adapted in the environment slowly over generations, not suddenly.

However, after Bretz's hypothesis started yielding magnitudes of evidence, geologists started to pay attention to this theory. In fact, other types of theories were only able to explain

하지만 제임스 하렌 브레츠라는 과학자는 그의 이 흥미로운 가설에 대한 분석을 전문 지질학자들의 협회에 제출했습니다. 그의 보고서에서 브레츠는 오늘날 미국의 북서쪽에 있는 워싱턴 주에 형성된 수로 암반 용암지대라고 불리는 독특한 풍경이 형성된 것에 대해 세부적으로 설명했습니다.

이 화산용암지대는 거대한 협곡과 거대한 폭포들을 포함하고 있었기 때문에 독특하게 여겨졌습니다. 그래서 전 세계를 통틀어서 이런 풍경은 어디에도 존재하지 않는다고 합니다. 그리고 지질학자들은 이것이 어떻게 형성되었는지에 대한 적절한 설명을 해내는 데 실패했습니다. 브레츠는 빙하기에 하룻밤 사이에 발생한 지질학적 대재앙인 거대한 홍수가 이러한 지형을 만들었다고 설명했습니다. 대부분 동일과정설 학자들의 견해를 공유하는 다른 유형의 가설도 있었습니다. 이 지질학자들은 점진적이고 반복적인 힘이 갑작스러운 변화를 만들 수 있을 만큼의 축적적인 힘으로 작용할 수 있다고 설명했습니다.

그러나 지속적인 연구는 화산용암지가 오랜 시간에 걸쳐 만들어졌다는 증거가 없다고 결론 내렸습니다. 하지만 많은 지질학자들은 동일과정설을 강하게 믿었기 때문에 그들은 그들의 믿음에 어긋난다는 이유로 이러한 이론들을 무시했습니다. 그들은 심지어 찰스 다윈이 동일과정설에 영향을 미친 것을 고려할 때, 그렇게 함으로써 지질학뿐 아니라 다른 과학도 살릴 수 있는 것이라고 생각하며 자신을 정당화했습니다. 다윈은 대부분의 생물들이 급작스럽게 변하는 게 아니라, 세대를 거쳐 서서히 환경에 적응하고 변화한다고 주장했습니다.

하지만, 브레츠의 가설이 이후로 수많은 증거들을 양산해내자, 지질학자들은 이 이론에 주목하기 시작했습니다. 실제로, 다른 유형의 이론들은 이 화산용암지대의 몇 가지 고립된 특징들만 설

certain isolated features of the scabland. On the other hand, Bretz's hypothesis was able to explain all the features of the scabland, and this was the main factor that persuaded other geologists. But that is not to say that we should disregard uniformitarianism. This means that we no longer strictly relied on the single theory of uniformitarianism and started paying attention to new possibilities of catastrophic events within the boundary of uniformitarianism.

You see, Bretz explained a huge flood occurred at the end of Ice Age due to a massive distant lake, created by a giant glacier that blocked the flow of water into the river. This glacier served as an ice dam that shut off the flow of water in and out of the lake for a very long time. After a long time had passed, the glacier started to break and melt due to the pressure coming from the lake and when the glacier finally broke the lake gave way to a huge flood that hit the northwestern part of the United States. Then these accumulating forces caused a sudden pressure, shaping the region we see today.

명할 수 있었습니다. 이와 다르게, 브레츠의 가설은 화산용암지대의 모든 특징들을 다 설명할 수 있었으며, 이것이 다른 지질학자들을 설득하는 주요한 요인이 되었습니다. 그렇다고 동일과정설를 무시해야 한다고 말하는 것은 아닙니다. 이것이 의미하는 것은 우리는 더 이상 동일과정설의 한 가지 이론에만 온전히 의존하지 않고, 동일과정설의 범위 안에서 새로운 급진적인 사건의 가능성에 대해 주의를 기울이기 시작했다는 것입니다.

브레츠는 빙하기의 끝에 거대한 빙하에 의해 물이 강으로 흘러가는 것이 막혀서 멀리 떨어진 호수로부터 거대한 홍수가 발생하였다고 설명했습니다. 이 빙하는 호수의 물이 흘러나가고 들어오는 것을 오랫동안 막는 얼음 댐의 역할을 했습니다. 오랜 시간이 지난 후, 호수에서 온 물의 압력 때문에 빙하가 부서지고 녹기 시작하였고, 빙하가 결국 완전히 부서졌을 때, 호수는 미국의 북서쪽을 강타한 홍수를 일으켰습니다. 그리고 이 축적된 힘은 급작스러운 압력을 야기했고, 오늘날 우리가 보는 지형의 형태로 깎아놓았습니다.

어휘_ modify 수정하다 intensity 강렬, 강도, 양 ridicule 비웃다, 조소하다 conference 협회 elaborate 자세히 말하다 channel 하상, 수로 canyon 협곡 neglect 무시하다 distant 멀리 떨어진

---

6. What is the main topic of the lecture?
Ⓐ Explaining the importance of uniformitarianism
Ⓑ Describing a theory about a previously inexplicable geological feature
Ⓒ Illustrating how uniformitarianists' neglected counteracting hypothesis
Ⓓ Proving the different theories concerning a geological feature

강의의 주된 주제는 무엇인가?
Ⓐ 동일과정설의 중요성을 설명하는 것
Ⓑ 종래의 설명할 수 없는 지질 특징에 관한 이론을 설명하는 것
Ⓒ 동일과정설 이론자들이 어떻게 반대되는 가설을 무시하는지 설명하는 것
Ⓓ 지형적인 특징을 설명하는 다양한 이론들을 증명하는 것

Listen again to a part of the conversation. Then answer the question.
대화의 일부분을 듣고 질문에 답하시오.

To rewind our conversation for a moment, uniformitarianism is one of the most basic guidelines of Geology that has been developed over 200 years. Given its solid foundation, how would you feel if someone challenged this long-standing theory?

우리의 강의를 잠시 떠올려보면, 동일과정설은 200년 이상 발전해온 지질학의 가장 기본적인 지침 중의 하나입니다. 그것의 튼튼한 기초를 감안할 때, 당신은 누군가가 이 오래된 이론에 도전한다면 어떻게 느끼시겠습니까?

7. What does the professor mean when he says this:

🎧 To rewind our conversation for a moment, uniformitarianism is one of the most basic guidelines of Geology that has been developed over 200 years.

Ⓐ He thinks the students missed a point he made earlier.

Ⓑ He realizes he forgot to mention something important.

Ⓒ He does not want the students to miss the key points.

Ⓓ He wants to return to a concept he referred to previously.

교수는 다음을 말할 때 무엇을 의미하는가: 우리의 강의를 잠시 떠올려보면, 동일과정설은 200년 이상 발전해온 지질학의 가장 기본적인 지침 중의 하나입니다.

Ⓐ 그는 그가 이전에 설명한 요점을 학생들이 놓쳤다고 생각한다.

Ⓑ 그는 중요한 부분을 언급하기를 까먹었다는 것을 깨달았디.

Ⓒ 그는 학생들이 요점들을 놓치는 것을 원하지 않는다.

Ⓓ 그는 앞에서 언급했던 개념으로 돌아가기를 원한다.

8. Why does the professor mention Charles Darwin?

Ⓐ To highlight that uniformitarianism was important in various fields

Ⓑ To provide an example of a scientist who invented uniformitarianism

Ⓒ To inform that Charles Darwin applied the concept of uniformitarianism to his research

Ⓓ To illustrate how uniformitarianism affected Charles Darwin

교수는 왜 찰스 다윈을 언급하는가?

Ⓐ 동일과정설이 다양한 분야에서 중요하다는 것을 강조하기 위해서

Ⓑ 동일과정설을 개발한 과학자의 예시를 들기 위해서

Ⓒ 찰스 다윈이 그의 연구에 동일과정설의 개념을 적용했다는 것을 알려주기 위해서

Ⓓ 동일과정설이 어떻게 찰스 다윈에게 영향을 줬는지를 설명하기 위해서

9. Why were the opponents to Bretz's hypothesis unable to discredit it? Click on 2 answers.

Ⓐ Bretz's hypothesis contained a lot of uniformitarianism concepts.

Ⓑ Bretz's hypothesis could only explain certain isolated parts of the scabland.

Ⓒ Bretz's hypothesis was used against a concept of uniformitarianism.

Ⓓ A lot of evidence was found in support of Bretz's hypothesis.

Ⓔ Bretz's hypothesis accounted for the entire formation of scabland geography.

브레츠의 가설의 반대자들이 왜 그것을 무효화할 수 없었는가? 정답을 2개 클릭하시오.

Ⓐ 브레츠의 가설은 많은 동일과정설 개념을 포함하고 있다.

Ⓑ 브레츠의 가설은 화산용암지대의 특정 고립된 부분만을 설명할 수 있다.

Ⓒ 브레츠의 가설은 동일과정설의 개념에 반대하는데 사용된다.

Ⓓ 브레츠의 가설을 지지하는 많은 증거들이 발견되었다.

Ⓔ 브레츠의 가설은 화산 지형의 전체적인 형성을 설명한다.

10. According to the professor's explanation at the end of the lecture, which one of the following describes the correct characteristic of the theory on how the channeled scabland was formed?

Ⓐ Uniformitarianism is the most accurate explanation for how the channeled scabland was gradually formed.

Ⓑ Bretz's theory is the most accurate explanation for how the channeled scabland as it was formed by a single catastrophic event.

Ⓒ Both uniformitarianism and Bretz's ideas did not correctly represent how the scabland was formed.

Ⓓ Both uniformitarianism and Bretz's ideas were correct, because the channeled scabland was formed by a series of catastrophic and gradual events.

강의 마지막에서 교수의 설명에 따르면, 다음 중 어떤 것이 화산용암지대가 어떻게 형성되었는지를 설명하는 이론의 올바른 특징을 묘사하고 있는가?

Ⓐ 동일과정설은 어떻게 수로 암반 용암지대가 점차적으로 형성됐는지에 대한 가장 정확한 설명이다.

Ⓑ 브레츠의 이론은 한 번의 재앙적인 사건으로 형성됐다는 수로 암반 용암지대에 대한 가장 정확한 설명이다.

Ⓒ 동일과정설과 브레츠의 이론 둘 다 어떻게 화산용암지대가 형성됐는지를 정확하게 설명하지 않는다.

Ⓓ 점차적인 사건들과 여러 번의 급격한 사건으로 수로 암반 용암지대가 형성됐기 때문에 동일과정설과 브레츠의 이론 둘 다 맞다.

Listen again to a part of the conversation. Then answer the question.
대화의 일부분을 듣고 질문에 답하시오.

On the other hand, Bretz's hypothesis was able to explain all the features of the scabland, and this was the main factor that persuaded other geologists. But that is not to say that we should disregard uniformitarianism.

이와 다르게, 브레츠의 가설은 화산용암지대의 모든 특징들을 다 설명할 수 있었고 이것이 다른 지질학자들을 설득하는 주요한 요인이 되었습니다. 그렇다고 동일과정설를 무시해야 한다고 말하는 것은 아닙니다.

11. What does the professor imply when he says this: 🎧 But that is not to say that we should disregard uniformitarianism.

- Ⓐ He's angry that many people ignore uniformitarianism.
- Ⓑ He thinks that people are responsible for disregarding uniformitarianism.
- Ⓒ He believes uniformitarianism is still acceptable to explain geological features.
- Ⓓ He wants to express his disdain for uniformitarianism.

교수가 다음과 같이 말할 때 무엇을 암시하는가: 그렇다고 동일과정설을 무시해야 한다고 말하는 것은 아닙니다.

- Ⓐ 그는 많은 사람들이 동일과정설을 무시하는 것에 화가 난다.
- Ⓑ 그는 사람들이 동일과정설을 무시하는 것에 책임이 있다고 생각한다.
- Ⓒ 그는 동일과정설이 지형적인 특징들을 설명하기 위해 아직까지 받아들여진다고 믿는다.
- Ⓓ 그는 동일과정설을 무시하는 자신의 감정을 표현하기를 원한다.

Part 2   Questions 12-17

12. Ⓑ	13. Ⓒ	14. Ⓐ	15. Ⓓ	16. Ⓐ	17. Ⓒ

[Questions 12-17] Listen to part of a lecture in an astronomy class.
천문학 수업의 강의 일부를 들으시오.

Test2_Listening_Part2_12-17.mp3

Technology is a valuable tool in various fields of science. Through the application of technology we can better observe and understand our universe. In particular, technology plays an important part in astronomy. When you think of astronomy, the first scientific instrument that pops into your head is probably the telescope. It's the best example of technology being used in astronomy. Okay, let me first explain the Hooker telescope. To me, it seems to be one of the most significant technological evolutions of the telescope. The Hooker telescope, which was the most powerful telescope available in the 1920s, allowed scientists to view the Milky Way as well as other galaxies. Thus, scientists could see that there were numerous galaxies, besides the Milky Way. Today, we take for granted that the Milky Way isn't the only galaxy in the universe, but back then that was an astonishing discovery. Another accomplishment of the Hooker telescope is that it led to the Big Bang theory. That is, it showed that

기술은 다양한 과학 분야에서 소중한 도구입니다. 기술을 적용함으로써, 우리는 우리의 우주를 더 잘 관찰하고 이해할 수 있죠. 특히, 기술은 천문학 분야에서 중요한 역할을 해요. 여러분이 천문학을 떠올렸을 때, 머릿속에 떠오르는 첫 번째 과학적 도구는 아마도 망원경일 거예요. 이것은 기술이 천문학에 쓰이는 가장 훌륭한 예죠. 좋아요, 우선 후커 망원경을 설명해보도록 할게요. 개인적으로, 저는 이것이 가장 중요한 망원경의 기술적 발전 중 하나라고 생각해요. 1920년대에 가장 강력했던 후커 망원경은 과학자들로 하여금 은하계뿐만 아니라 다른 은하계도 관찰할 수 있도록 해주었어요. 따라서 과학자들은 저 밖에 은하수 말고도 수많은 은하계가 존재함을 알 수 있었겠죠. 오늘날 우리는 은하수가 우주에서 유일한 은하계가 아님을 당연하게 생각하지만, 그 당시에, 그것은 매우 놀라운 발견이었어요. 후커 망원경의 또 다른 업적은 그것이 빅뱅이론을 세우는 데 기여했다는 것입니다. 즉, 망원경은 은하계가 서로로부터 멀어지고 있다는 것을 보여주었습니다.

the galaxies were moving away from one another, going farther and farther away.

What is the Big Bang theory? As most of us already know, this theory proposes that the universe exploded into existence about 15 billion years ago. In a huge explosion, everything in the universe blew apart in different directions, a situation that is still ongoing. It's a revolutionary theory that has completely changed the way we view the universe. And this dramatic shift of perspective was, in part, brought by the Hooker telescope. Now, let's talk about a more current technological tool: the interferometer. It's a special kind of large telescope, made by linking 2 or more telescopes together. It's used to observe starlight, which it captures and sends down tubes or pipes. The tubes are connected to computers that compile all of the images into one single image.

Of course that's a bit of a simplification, but I hope the basic concept is clear. By the way, the early interferometer consisted mostly of two telescopes that measured power on a small angular scale. These two telescopes were usually identical. As the interferometer developed through time, it became more complex. A lot of modern interferometers utilize 6 telescopes, wired with pipes that send images back to computers. Upon receiving the images, scientists synchronize them so that it makes a complete and accurate depiction. In reality, it's an extremely complicated process that requires high technical skill. Despite the level of work involved, it's all worth it, because interferometers produce better images than traditional telescopes. Although interferometers don't help us see farther, they give us images that are up to 50 times sharper than conventional telescopes. Not surprisingly, bigger telescopes have better resolution… and also cost more.

While interferometers have some disadvantages, the sharp pictures they produce are very useful.

빅뱅이론이 뭐죠? 여러분 대부분이 알듯이 이것은 우주가 150억 년 전에 폭발하여 생겼다는 이론이에요. 이 거대한 폭발 과정에서, 우주에 있던 모든 것이 서로 다른 방향으로 산산이 흩어졌어요. 이 과정은 현재진행형이고요. 이것은 우주를 보는 관점을 완전히 변화시킨 혁신적인 이론입니다. 그리고 이 극적인 관점의 변화는, 부분적으로, 후커 망원경에 의해 이루어졌고요. 그럼 이제, 조금 더 최신의 기술 도구인 간섭계에 관해 이야기해보도록 하죠. 이것은 두 개 이상의 망원경을 함께 연결시켜 만든 특별한 종류의 큰 망원경입니다. 이것은 별빛을 관찰하는 데 쓰입니다. 별빛을 포착해서 튜브나 관으로 보내죠. 그 튜브들은 모든 이미지를 조합해 하나의 이미지를 만들어내는 컴퓨터와 연결되어 있어요.

물론, 이것은 꽤 간단화시킨 거예요. 하지만 기본 개념은 이해했으면 합니다. 초기의 간섭계는 대부분 각진 작은 저울로 힘을 측정하는 두 개의 망원경으로 구성되었죠. 이 두 개의 망원경은 대개 동일했고요. 간섭계가 발전하면서, 그것은 더욱 복잡해졌어요. 많은 최신식 간섭계는 컴퓨터로 이미지를 전송하는 파이프로 연결된 여섯 개의 망원경을 이용합니다. 이 이미지들을 전송받으면, 과학자들은 그 이미지들을 조합하여 그것이 최대한 완전하고 정확한 묘사가 되도록 만들죠. 실제로, 이것은 높은 기술을 요하는 매우 복잡한 과정이에요. 이런 난이도의 작업이 필요함에도, 이것은 충분한 가치가 있어요. 왜냐하면 간섭계는 옛날의 망원경들보다 더 나은 이미지를 만들어내기 때문이에요. 간섭계가 우리가 더 먼 곳을 보는 것에 도움이 되진 않더라도, 그들은 이전의 망원경들보다 50배나 선명한 이미지를 제공해줘요. 별로 놀랍지 않게도, 망원경이 클수록 더 좋은 해상도를 지니죠… 그리고 물론 가격도 더 나가고요.

간섭계가 몇 개의 단점을 지닐지라도, 그들이 생산해내는 선명한 사진들은 매우 유용해요. 예를

For example, do you remember how we observed Castor in the Gemini constellation last week? When we used the traditional telescope, Castor looked like a fuzzy star. But with an interferometer, what happened? We could tell that Castor actually had 6 stars orbiting one another, resembling something like a wild dance. This relates to a phenomenon in the universe. In our solar system the sun is one large star. It exerts strong gravitational force on other components of the universe and each planet or celestial body with a large density attract satellites to itself. Using this sophisticated machine, we can attain better knowledge about astronomical bodies in outer space.

More importantly than being able to observe stars, however, is the next benefit that advanced telescopes have; we can utilize them to find more planets! Since the interferometer gives us accurate images of things that were previously blurry or unclear, we have a better chance of identifying more planets. You see, it's possible that conventional telescopes could have missed some, due to their low resolution. With interferometers, we can find new planets and one of them may even have life. It doesn't have to be intelligent life present on the planet – the discovery of any kind of life, however basic, will be a scientific breakthrough.

Oh, but don't let that sound like I'm putting down the Hooker telescope. Without the Hooker telescope, we wouldn't know about the Milky Way or the expanding galaxies. We're all familiar with the Big Bang theory and how it's altered our view of the universe. Just like the interferometer, the Hooker telescope gave us a new perspective about the universe. "Well, once the interferometer finds a planet with life, then that comparison is subject to change."

들면, 여러분, 우리가 저번 주에 어떻게 쌍둥이자리에 있는 카스토르를 관측했는지 기억하나요? 우리가 예전 망원경을 이용했을 때, 카스토르는 흐릿한 별로 보였어요. 하지만 간섭계를 이용하였을 때 무슨 일이 일어났나요? 우리는 카스토르가 실제로 그것의 주위를 도는 6개의 별을 가지고 있었고, 그것들은 거친 춤과 비슷한 모양으로 움직인다는 것을 알 수 있었죠. 이것은 우주 현상과 관련됩니다. 우리의 태양계에서, 우리의 태양은 하나의 큰 별이에요. 강한 중력의 힘으로 우주의 물질들을 잡아당기고, 각각의 행성이나 무게가 큰 천체들은 각각의 독립적인 힘으로 주변의 작은 위성들을 달고 있어요. 이 정교한 기계를 통해서 우리는 천체에 대한 더 자세한 정보를 좀 더 분명하게 얻을 수 있답니다.

별들을 관찰할 수 있는 것보다 중요한 것은, 진보된 망원경들은 또 다른 장점들도 가지고 있다는 거예요. 우리는 그들을 더 많은 행성들을 찾는 데 쓸 수 있습니다! 원래 흐릿하거나 잘 안보였던 것들의 이미지를 간섭계가 더 명확하게 보여줌으로써, 우리는 더 많은 행성들을 발견할 기회를 갖게 돼요. 자, 보면, 전통적인 망원경은 해상도가 낮기 때문에 몇 개의 행성들을 발견하지 못했을 수도 있어요. 하지만 간섭계를 사용함으로써, 우리는 새로운 행성들을 찾을 수 있어요. 그들 중 하나는 생명체를 가지고 있을지도 모르지요. 지적 능력이 있는 생물이 아니어도 괜찮아요. 새로운 생명체의 발견은 그것이 얼마나 원시적이든지 과학적인 혁신이 될 겁니다.

오, 하지만 제가 이런 말을 한다고 후커 망원경을 등한시한다고 생각하지는 마세요. 후커 망원경이 없었다면, 우리는 은하수나 팽창하는 은하계를 알 수 없었을 겁니다. 우리 모두가 빅뱅이론에 익숙하고 그것이 어떻게 우리가 우주를 바라보는 관점을 바꿨는지 알고 있지요. 간섭계와 마찬가지로, 후커 망원경은 우주에 대한 새로운 관점을 우리에게 제공해줬어요. 그렇지만, 일단 간섭계가 생명체가 살고 있는 행성을 발견한다면, 뭐 이 두 가지 기술의 비교는 바뀔 수도 있겠네요.

12. What does the professor primarily discuss?
Ⓐ The Big Bang Theory and its scientific importance
Ⓑ Astronomical techniques in astronomythat shaped our perspective of the universe
Ⓒ The contrast between two competing types of telescopes
Ⓓ Various rolesof computers in producing high-resolution images

교수는 주로 무엇에 대하여 이야기하는가?
Ⓐ 빅뱅이론과 그것이 과학적으로 가지는 중요성
Ⓑ 우주에 대한 우리의 시각을 형성한 천문학의 기술들
Ⓒ 두 개의 뛰어난 종류의 망원경들에 대한 대조
Ⓓ 고해상도 이미지를 만들어내는 데 컴퓨터가 하는 다양한 역할들

13. Why is the hooker telescope important?
Ⓐ It showed the creation of the Milky Way and other galaxies.
Ⓑ It was the most sophisticated telescope in the 1930s.
Ⓒ It aided the development of the Big Bang theory.
Ⓓ It utilized several telescopes and computers.

후커 망원경이 왜 중요한가?
Ⓐ 그것은 은하수와 다른 은하계의 탄생을 보여주었다.
Ⓑ 그것은 1930년대에 존재했던 가장 복잡한 망원경이다.
Ⓒ 그것은 빅뱅이론의 발전에 기여했다.
Ⓓ 그것은 여러 개의 망원경들과 컴퓨터들을 이용하였다.

Listen again to a part of the conversation. Then answer the question.
대화의 일부분을 듣고 질문에 답하시오.

Of course that's a bit of a simplification, but I hope the basic concept is clear. By the way, the early interferometer consisted mostly of two telescopes that measured power on a small angular scale.

물론, 이것은 꽤 간단화시킨 거예요. 하지만 기본 개념은 이해했으면 합니다. 초기의 간섭계는 대부분 각진 작은 저울로 힘을 측정하는 두 개의 망원경으로 구성되었죠.

14. What does the professor imply when he says this: 🎧 Of course, That's a bit of a simplification, but I hope the basic concept is clear.
Ⓐ He omitted some of the more difficult and complex ideas.
Ⓑ The students should review their lecture notes carefully.
Ⓒ The students should study the concept on their own time.
Ⓓ He thinks that the students cannot understand the telescope because of its complexity.

교수가 이 말을 할 때, 무엇을 암시하는가?: 물론, 이것은 꽤 간단화시킨 거예요. 하지만 기본 개념은 이해했으면 합니다.
Ⓐ 그는 더 어렵고 복잡한 개념들을 생략했다.
Ⓑ 학생들은 자신의 강의 노트들을 주의 깊게 보는 것이 좋다.
Ⓒ 학생들은 이 개념을 스스로 공부하는 것이 좋다.
Ⓓ 그는 학생들이 망원경의 복잡함 때문에 이것을 이해하지 못한다고 생각한다.

15. According to the professor, why is it difficult to create an image with an interferometer?

Ⓐ Pipes connecting the telescopes with computers are thousands of meters long.

Ⓑ Telescopes require frequent and expensive maintenance.

Ⓒ Telescope operators lack sufficient knowledge about imaging computers.

Ⓓ Multiple images have to be synchronized into one complete image.

교수의 말에 의하면, 간섭계를 이용해서 이미지를 만드는 것이 왜 복잡한가?

Ⓐ 망원경과 컴퓨터를 연결하는 관이 수천 미터 길이이다.

Ⓑ 망원경은 종종 비싼 유지비를 필요로 한다.

Ⓒ 망원경 조작자는 컴퓨터로 이미지 작업하는 것에 관한 지식이 부족하다.

Ⓓ 여러 개의 이미지들이 하나의 완전한 이미지로 합쳐져야 한다.

16. Why does the professor mention their observation of Castor?

Ⓐ To point out an advantage of advanced technology

Ⓑ To bring up a problem with conventional telescopes

Ⓒ To note the presence of multiple stars in some celestial bodies

Ⓓ To emphasize the importance of the 6 surrounding stars

왜 교수는 카스토르 관찰을 언급했는가?

Ⓐ 진보된 기술이 가져다주는 장점을 강조하기 위해

Ⓑ 이전의 망원경이 가졌던 문제를 제시하기 위해

Ⓒ 몇 개의 천체에 있는 다양한 별들의 존재를 알리기 위해

Ⓓ 주변에서 발견한 6개의 별의 중요성을 강조하기 위해

Listen again to a part of the conversation. Then answer the question.
대화의 일부분을 듣고 질문에 답하시오.

Just like the interferometer, the Hooker telescope gave us a new perspective about the universe. "Well, once the interferometer finds a planet with life, then that comparison is subject to change."

후커 망원경은 우주에 대한 새로운 관점을 우리에게 제공해줬어요. 그렇지만, 일단 간섭계가 생명체가 살고 있는 행성을 발견한다면, 뭐 이 두 가지 기술의 비교는 바뀔 수도 있겠네요.

17. What does the professor imply when he says this: 🎧 "Well, once the interferometer finds a planet with life, then that comparison is subject to change."

Ⓐ The next lecture will be about the sustenance of life on other planets.

Ⓑ The professor expects students to understand the meaning of life on Earth.

Ⓒ The professor thinks the advanced technology could result in scientific progress.

Ⓓ The professor emphasizes the importance of the particular discovery.

교수는 이런 말을 했을 때 무엇을 암시하는가?: 그렇지만, 일단 간섭계가 생명체가 살고 있는 행성을 발견한다면, 뭐 이 두 가지 기술의 비교는 바뀔 수도 있겠네요.

Ⓐ 다음 수업 시간의 주제는 다른 행성에서의 생명의 자양물을 다룰 것이다.

Ⓑ 교수는 학생들이 지구에 생명이 존재하는 것의 의미를 알아차리길 바란다.

Ⓒ 교수는 진보된 기술이 과학적 진보를 이끌 수 있을 것이라고 생각한다.

Ⓓ 교수는 이 특정한 발견의 중요성을 강조하고 있다.

Question 1 / 6

Question Among intelligence, creativity and courage, what is the most important quality that a student should have? State your opinion and explain why.

해 석 지성, 창의력, 용기 중 학생이 가져야 하는 가장 중요한 자질은 무엇인가? 당신의 의견을 말하고 설명하시오.

Sample Note-taking

courage

　　1) meet ≒ ppl + gain exp

　　　→ exp s.n. + br persp

　　2) ins 2 make eff

　　　→ conc ↑

Sample Answer

Test2_Speaking_1_Sample.mp3

As **far** as I'm con**cer**ned, / I **stro**ngly think / **cou**rage is the **mo**st important **qua**lity / that a **stu**dent should have. /

There are **two** reasons for this. /

The **fir**st reason is / that **tho**se who have a lot of **cou**rage / can have the oppor**tu**nity to **meet** different people / and gain **va**luable experiences / that they've **ne**ver known before. / This would **allo**w them to ex**pa**nd their **so**cial networks / and **broa**den their perspectives, / and it **e**ven makes them com**pe**titive / in the **fu**ture job market. /

The **se**cond reason is / that being **self**-confident / ins**pir**es people / to make **mo**re effort / and become res**pon**sible. / Then **stu**dents would be able to **con**centrate **be**tter on their studies. / This can **br**ing about / **be**tter outcomes at schools. /

 내가 생각하기에, 학생이 지녀야 할 가장 중요한 자질은 용기이다.

여기엔 두 가지 이유가 있다.

첫 번째 이유로, 용기 있는 사람들은 다양한 사람들을 만날 기회가 있고 그들이 전엔 알지 못했던 값진 경험을 할 수 있다. 이것은 그들의 사회적 네트워크와 관점을 넓혀줄 것이다.

두 번째 이유는 자신에 대해 자신감을 가지는 것이 더 많은 노력과 책임감을 가지도록 동기부여를 하기 때문이다. 그렇게 되면 그들은 자신의 일에 더 집중할 수 있을 것이다. 이것은 직장이나 학교에서 더 나은 결과를 이끌어낼 수 있다.

Question 2 / 6

Question **Would you prefer to constantly move around from one place to another, or to live in one place for a long time? Give your opinion and explain why.**

해 석 당신은 여러 장소를 지속적으로 옮겨다니며 사는 것을 선호하는가, 아니면 한 장소에서 오래 사는 것을 선호하는가? 의견을 말하고, 설명하시오.

Sample Note-taking

```
move around

  1) meet ≈ ppl + gain exp

    → exp s.n. + br persp

  2) ins 2 make eff

    → conc ↑
```

Sample Answer

Test2_Speaking_2_Sample.mp3

As **far** as I'm con**cer**ned, / I **stro**ngly prefer / to **con**stantly move ar**ou**nd / from **one** place to an**o**ther. /

There are **two** reasons for this. /

The **fir**st reason is / that moving ar**ou**nd / from **one** place to an**o**ther / makes it **po**ssible / for me to talk about **dif**ferent things in life / and gain **va**luable experiences / that I've

never **kno**wn before. / This allows me to en**han**ce my **so**cial network / and **broa**den my pers**pec**tive. /

The **se**cond reason is / that **mee**ting different people and **tal**king to them / will ins**pire** me to make **mo**re effort / and become res**pon**sible / for what I **do**. / Then I am able to **con**centrate **bet**ter at work. / This can **bri**ng about / a **bet**ter outcome. /

해석 내가 생각하기에, 나는 한 곳에서 다른 곳으로 지속적으로 이동하는 것을 선호한다.

여기엔 두 가지 이유가 있다.

첫 번째로, 이곳에서 저곳으로 이사하는 것은 다양한 사람들을 만나고 이전엔 몰랐던 값진 경험들을 하게 한다. 이것은 내가 사회적 네트워크와 관점을 넓힐 수 있게 해준다.

두 번째로, 다른 사람들을 만나고 그들과 대화하는 것은 내가 더 노력하고 내 일에 있어서 더 책임감 있는 사람이 되도록 자극한다. 그러면 나는 일에 더 집중할 수 있다. 이것은 더 나은 결과를 이끌어낸다.

Question 3 / 6

Question The woman expresses her opinion about the announcement. State her opinion and explain the reasons why she feels that way.

해 석 여자는 공지사항에 대해서 본인의 의견을 밝혔다. 그녀의 의견과 그렇게 느끼는 이유를 설명하시오.

Sample Reading Note-taking

R: stds have to find own housing off campus

Sample Listening Note-taking

W: O

R 1: cheaper if apt self

　　ex) sister

　　　- 'willing 2 host' tab on web

R 2: use Sp. often

- learn lang + culture

- if in dorm → use Eng all day

- practice, fluent

Sample Answer

According to the announcement, / the university decided / that students who want to study abroad in Spain / need to find their own housing. /

The woman thinks / the announcement is a great idea, / and she gives two reasons / for holding her opinion. /

The first reason she mentions / is that students can find / cheaper apartments. / For example, / her sister went study abroad, / and she told her / that students can find cheap and nice apartments / on the school website. /

The second reason she mentions / is that students will be able to learn Spanish / this way. / This is because / students go study abroad to learn the language / and the culture. / So if they just live in dorms / with other students who speak English / they will only be using English / all day. /

So for these reasons, / she thinks this announcement / is a good idea. /

해석 공지에 따르면 학교는 스페인에서 공부하려는 학생들이 그들 자신의 숙소를 스스로 구해야 할 것을 결정했다.

여자는 이 공지가 좋은 계획이라고 생각한다. 그래서 그녀는 자신의 의견을 뒷받침할 두 가지 이유를 말한다.

그녀가 말한 첫 번째 이유는 학생들이 더 저렴한 아파트를 구할 수 있기 때문이다. 예를 들자면, 그녀의 언니가 외국에서 공부를 했었는데, 학생들이 학교 홈페이지를 통해서 저렴하고 좋은 아파트를 구할 수 있다고 말했다.

그녀가 말한 두 번째 이유는, 학생들이 스스로 지낼 곳을 알아보면서 스페인어를 배울 수 있기 때문이다. 학생들은 언어와 문화를 배우기 위해 유학을 간다. 그래서 만약 영어를 하는 다른 학생들과 기숙사에서만 지낸다면 하루 종일 영어만 쓰게 될 것이다.

이런 이유들로 그녀는 이 공지가 좋은 결정이라고 생각한다.

Reading

New Policy for Study Abroad Programs in Spain

One of our school's most popular study abroad programs is at Madrid University in Spain. However, there have been some changes for this program. As most of you already know, students who studied abroad in Madrid University were guaranteed a dormitory room. However, from now on students will have to find their own housing off campus. The number of students who wish to live on campus has increased at Madrid University, so they are saying that they cannot provide dorms for study abroad students as well. We hope the students consider this change in policy before applying for the study abroad program to Spain.

스페인 유학 프로그램을 위한 새로운 정책

우리 학교에서 가장 인기 많은 유학 프로그램 중 하나는 스페인의 마드리드대학으로 가는 것이다. 그러나 이 프로그램에 몇 가지 변화가 생겼다. 대부분의 사람들이 알듯이, 마드리드대학에서 유학하는 학생들은 기숙사가 보장됐다. 하지만 이제부터 학생들은 학교 밖에서 집을 찾아야 한다. 마드리드대학교 내에서 살고 싶어 하는 학생들의 수가 늘어서 학교는 유학생들에게 기숙사를 더 이상 제공하지 못하게 되었다고 말한다. 우리는 학생들이 스페인 유학 프로그램에 신청하기 전에 이 정책 변경을 고려했으면 한다.

Listening Script

`Test2_Speaking_3_Sample.mp3`

M Did you see the changes in the policy for studying abroad in Spain?

W I did.

M I thought I should tell you since I remember you saying that you were going to Spain next semester.

W I am actually glad the policy changed before I go.

M Really? Why is that? I thought it was more expensive to live off campus.

W Actually it could be cheaper if I find an apartment all by myself. My sister told me that there was a "willing to host" tab on the university website, where you can find cheap and nice appartment.

M That is nice. Your sister stayed in Madrid too?

M 스페인 유학 프로그램 정책의 변화에 대해 봤니?

W 응.

M 네가 다음 학기에 스페인 간다고 했던 게 기억나서 너한테 말해줘야 한다고 생각했어.

W 내가 가기 전에 정책이 바뀌어서 다행이야.

M 정말? 왜? 나는 학교 밖에 사는 게 더 비쌀 거라고 생각했는데.

W 내가 혼자 아파트를 찾으면 더 쌀 수도 있어. 우리 언니가 학교 웹사이트에 '호스트할 의향 있음'이라는 탭이 있다고 말해줬어. 거기에서 싸고 좋은 아파트를 찾을 수 있대.

M 좋네. 네 언니도 마드리드에 있었어?

W She did. I also think this policy is a good idea since it will help me use Spanish more often. As you know, most students go on study abroad programs to learn the language and culture of that country.

M Right.

W If I stay in the dormitory with other people who speak English, I would barely have a chance to speak Spanish. I will be using English all day.

M I guess that is true. If you live off campus, you will have to use Spanish, first when you are trying to find an apartment, and also whenever you need to buy or repair something.

W That would really be a lot of practice. I want to become fluent in Spanish while I am there.

M It seems like a policy that fits you well then!

W Definitely. I am happy with it. I can't wait to go to Spain.

W 응. 또 내가 스페인어를 더 자주 사용하게 도와줄 것 같아서 이 정책이 좋은 아이디어라고 생각해. 너도 알다시피, 대부분의 학생들은 그 나라의 언어와 문화를 배우기 위해 유학을 가잖아.

M 그렇지.

W 기숙사에서 영어를 쓰는 다른 사람들과 지낸다면 스페인어를 말할 기회가 거의 없을 거야. 영어를 하루 종일 쓰겠지.

M 맞는 말이야. 학교 밖에서 살면, 아파트를 찾을 때나 뭔가를 사거나 고칠 때마다 스페인어를 사용해야 할거야.

W 정말 많은 연습이 될 거야. 거기에서 스페인어를 유창하게 하고 싶어.

M 이 정책은 너한테 딱 맞아 보여!

W 맞아. 나는 정말 기뻐. 스페인을 빨리 가고 싶어.

Question 4 / 6

Question Using points and examples from the lecture, explain what occam's razor is.

해 석 강의의 예시를 사용해서 오컴의 면도날이 무엇인지 설명하시오.

Sample Reading Note-taking

occam's razor

- the best solution to a problem is usually the simplest solution

Sample Listening Note-taking

```
ex) 1 day – car: flat tire

1 conc: hate you?

    - followed → waited till gone → stabbed 2

    // why X 4?

    - how X see him

2 conc:

    - broken glass

    → drove over

        ⇨ Simplest sol. : best
```

Sample Answer

In the **le**cture, / the pro**fe**ssor talks about / **o**ccam's **ra**zor. (**O**ccam's razor states / that the **be**st solution to a **pro**blem / is **usu**ally the **sim**plest solution.)

The pro**fe**ssor gives an e**xa**mple. /

Say, **o**ne day / you **fou**nd out that your **car** has **fla**t tires. / So you **try** to think / why this **ha**ppened to you. / Then you come **up** with **two** conclusions. /

The **fir**st conclusion / is that **so**meone that **ha**tes you / **did** this. / Speci**fi**cally, he fo**ll**owed you ar**oun**d / and **wait**ed until you were **go**ne. / Then he **sta**bbed **two** tires. /

The **se**cond conclusion / is that you remember there were **bro**ken glasses, / and you drove **o**ver them. /

What he **men**tioned in the lecture / is that out of the **two** conclusions, / the **se**cond one is **be**tter. / **This** is because / the **sim**plest solution is the **best** one./

해석 강의에서 교수는 오컴의 면도날에 대해서 설명한다. (오컴의 면도날은 어떤 문제에 있어서 가장 간단한 것이 가장 좋은 해결책임을 말한다.)

교수는 예시를 든다.

가령, 어느 날 당신의 차 타이어에 구멍이 난 것을 발견했다고 해보자. 그래서 왜 이 일이 당신에게 생겼는지 생각해본다. 당신은 두 가지의 결론에 다다른다.

첫 번째는 당신을 싫어하는 누군가가 한 짓이라는 것이다. 상세히 말하자면, 그 사람이 따라와서 당신이 사라지기를 기다렸다가 그 다음에 두 타이어를 찌른다.

두 번째는 길 위에 부서진 유리조각들이 있었고 당신은 그 위를 운전해 지나갔다는 것을 기억해냈다는 것이다.

교수는 강의에서 두 개의 결론 중 두 번째가 더 낫다고 말한다. 왜냐하면 가장 단순한 방법이 가장 좋은 방법이기 때문이다.

Reading

Occam's Razor

In the late 1300s and early 1400s, there was a Franciscan monk named William of Occam. Throughout his life, he was part of a number of papal controversies, but these days he is most remembered for a principle called Occam's razor. William of Occam is not the person who created the principle, but he has become famously associated with it because he used it. This principle proposes that if a person is presented with a problem, he should "shave" all unnecessary factors to solve it. Basically, Occam's razor states that the best solution to a problem is usually the simplest solution.

오컴의 면도날

1300년대 후기와 1400년대 초기에, 윌리엄 오브 오컴이라는 성 프란체스코의 수도사 한 명이 있었습니다. 그의 삶 동안에, 그는 교황 제도의 많은 논쟁의 일부분이었는데 요새는 오컴의 면도날이라 불리는 원리로 가장 많이 기억됩니다. 윌리엄 오브 오컴은 이 원리를 창안해낸 사람은 아니지만, 이와 유명하게 연관되었는데 그 이유는 그가 이것을 사용했기 때문입니다. 이 원리는 어떤 사람이 문제에 봉착했을 때, 그 문제를 풀기 위해 모든 불필요한 요소들을 '제거해야' 한다고 제안합니다. 기본적으로, 오컴의 면도날은 문제에 대해 가장 좋은 해결책은 보통 가장 단순한 해결책이라고 기술합니다.

Listening Script

I'm going to give you an example of how thinking too much can be a bad thing. Let me present you with a situation. One day, you go outside to find that your car has two flat tires. You take your car to the shop and get it fixed with new ones and then, you start to wonder what happened to make the tires go flat. You come up with two possible answers.

너무 많이 생각하는 것이 나쁜 일이 될 수도 있다는 것에 대한 예를 들어보겠습니다. 상황 하나를 드리겠습니다. 어느 날, 여러분은 밖에 나가서 차의 타이어 두 개가 바람이 빠졌다는 것을 알게 됩니다. 차를 가게로 옮겨 새것으로 고칩니다. 그리고 나서, 여러분은 무엇이 타이어에 구멍을 냈는지 궁금해합니다. 여러분은 아마 두 가지 답을 생각하게 될 것입니다.

Your first conclusion is that someone walked by and poked holes in your tires. You try to figure out why someone would do this to your car. Is there someone that hates you that much? Maybe you accidentally made someone mad on your way to work, and he followed you until you stopped.

Next, he waited until you were gone and then stabbed two of your tires. But wait, why didn't he cut all four tires? And how did he do this without anyone seeing him? You were parked in a busy area, so someone would have reported him.

Then, you come to a second conclusion. You remember that there was some broken glass on the street when you were driving to work. You must have accidentally driven over the glass and popped two tires without realizing it. Pretty simple, right? What sounds more likely; someone followed you and slashed two tires, or you accidentally drove over some glass and popped two tires?

I think it's the simplest choice. The first one is too complicated and just sounds unlikely. Usually, the simplest solution turns out to be the best one.

첫 번째 결론은 누군가 걸어가다 타이어에 구멍을 냈다는 것입니다. 누군가가 왜 이런 일을 했을지 밝혀내려 합니다. 당신을 몹시 싫어하는 사람이 있는 걸까요? 어쩌면 당신은 출근길에 우연히 누군가를 화나게 만들었고 그는 당신이 멈출 때까지 따라왔습니다.

그 다음에, 당신이 갈 때까지 기다렸고 타이어 두 개를 찔렀습니다. 그렇지만, 그는 왜 네 개의 타이어 모두 자르지 않았을까요? 그리고 누구에게도 목격당하지 않고 어떻게 했을까요? 혼잡한 지역에 주차했으니까 누군가 그를 신고했을 텐데 말이죠.

그리고, 여러분은 두 번째 결론에 다다릅니다. 출근하기 위해 운전하고 있을 때 거리에 깨진 유리들이 있었음을 기억합니다. 당신은 우연히 유리 위로 운전했고 미처 깨닫지 못하고 타이어 두 개를 터뜨렸을 것입니다. 꽤 단순하지 않습니까? 누군가 여러분을 따라온 후 타이어 두 개를 긋는 것. 또는 여러분이 유리 위로 잘못 운전하여 타이어 두 개를 터뜨린 것. 이 둘 중에 어느 것이 더 가능성 있게 들리나요?

제 생각에 이건 간단한 선택입니다. 첫 번째는 너무 복잡하고 정말 비현실적으로 들려요. 보통, 가장 간단한 해결책이 가장 좋은 것으로 판명됩니다.

Question The woman expresses her feelings about the problem. What is the problem and what are the suggestions that were made? What do you think the woman should do?

해 석 여자는 문제점에 대해서 의견을 말한다. 문제점이 무엇이고, 제시된 해결책이 무엇인가? 당신은 여자가 어떻게 해야 된다고 생각하는가?

Sample Listening Note-taking

M	W
	P: get published
	write p – on journal
	// lim. on length
S 1. shorten	
+ X how long wait	- shorten half, 1/2 the original
S 2. wait till sum. pub	
+ another chance	
	- std + prof on vac.
	→ X read

Sample Answer

`Test2_Speaking_5_Sample.mp3`

The **wo**man's problem is / that she **wa**nts to publish her paper / on the **schoo**l journal, / but the **e**ditor is **as**king her / to **sho**rten it. /

The **man** and the woman / come up with **two** possible solutions / for the **pro**blem. /

The **fir**st one is / to just **sho**rten the paper, / and the **se**cond one is / to **wa**it for the **su**mmer publi**ca**tion. / I think / the **wo**man should choose the **fir**st solution. /

The **fir**st reason is / that **not** a lot of **peo**ple / will be able to **read** her paper / if her **pa**per is **pu**blished / in the **su**mmer publication. /

The **se**cond reason is / that she may **have** to **sho**rten it **any**way / for the **su**mmer publication. /

So **the**se are the reasons / why she should **go** with the **fir**st solution. /

해석 여자의 문제는 그녀가 논문을 발표하고 싶어 하는데 편집자가 논문을 줄여달라고 요청한 것이다.

남자와 여자는 이 문제에 대해 2가지 가능한 해결책을 생각한다.

첫 번째는 논문을 줄이는 것이고 두 번째는 여름 출간까지 기다리는 것이다. 나는 여자가 첫 번째 방법을 선택해야 한다고 생각한다.

첫 번째 이유는 만약 그녀가 여름에 출간한다면 많은 사람들이 그녀의 논문을 읽을 수 없을 것이기 때문이다.

두 번째 이유는 여름 출간을 위해서도 어차피 논문을 줄여야 하기 때문이다.

이런 이유로 나는 그녀가 첫 번째 방법을 선택해야 한다고 생각한다.

Listening Script

Test2_Speaking_5_Listening.mp3

M How are you doing on your essay? I heard that you were trying to get it published.

W Yes. I am writing a big paper on the history of our university. I am trying to publish it in the school journal.

M I see. I remember the editor saying that there is a limitation on the paper's length.

W That is where I am stuck. The editor wants me to shorten the paper or else I will have to publish it some other time.

M Can't you just try shortening your paper? You never know how long you would have to wait if you miss this chance.

W That is true, but I have to shorten it to almost half the length of the original. I worked on it for so long, so it is very difficult for me to delete everything.

M I understand your feelings. How about waiting until the summer to publish your paper? Although it is quite far away, I am sure you will have another chance in the summer publication.

W I did think of that option as well, but as you

M 에세이는 어떻게 되어가고 있어? 네가 그것을 출판하려 한다고 들었어.

W 응. 우리 학교의 역사에 대해 중요한 논문을 쓰고 있어. 학교 학술지에 게재하려고 해.

M 그렇구나. 논문의 길이에 제한이 있다고 편집장이 말했던 게 기억나.

W 그 부분이 지금 내가 막혀 있는 데야. 편집장은 내가 논문을 줄이길 원해. 아니면 나는 다른 때에 게재해야 해.

M 그냥 논문을 줄이면 안 돼? 이번 기회를 놓치면 얼마나 기다려야 할지 모르잖아.

W 맞는 말이야. 하지만 원본에 비해 거의 반절로 줄여야 해. 너무 오랫동안 작업해서 삭제하기가 정말 힘들어.

M 네 기분 이해 해. 그러면 논문 게재를 여름까지 기다려보는 건 어때? 꽤 많이 남았지만 여름 발행 때 한 번 더 기회가 있을 거라고 확신해.

W 그 옵션도 생각해봤어. 하지만 너도 알다시피 대부분의 학생들과 교수님

know, most of the students and professors leave campus in the summer to go on vacation. Not many people will be able to read my article since they won't be here. I want as many people to read my work as possible.

M This really is a dilemma, isn't it? I hope you think it over carefully before making your decision.

W Thanks.

M Wish you luck! I hope to read your article soon.

들은 여름에 휴가를 가느라 캠퍼스를 떠나. 많은 사람들이 이곳에 없어서 내 기사를 읽지 못할 거야. 나는 최대한 많은 사람들이 내 글을 읽었으면 좋겠어.

M 이거 정말 딜레마네? 네가 신중히 생각해보고 결정했으면 좋겠어.

W 고마워.

M 행운을 빌어! 네 기사를 곧 읽었으면 좋겠어.

Question 6 / 6

Question Using points and examples from the lecture, discuss the two ways sea creatures obtain nutrition in the deep ocean.

해 석 강의의 예시를 이용하여, 심해에서 바다 생물들이 영양분을 얻는 두가지 방법에 대해서 설명하시오.

Sample Listening Note-taking

```
Topic: fixed dwellers - live bottom of ocean fl.

  1 w: active method

    ex) anemones: tentacles

      - paralyze fish

      → keep healthy

  2 w: passive method

    ex) oysters: X move

      - allow ocean current flow

      - filter out nut. & obtain

      // effective
```

Sample Answer

In the **lec**ture, / the pro**fe**ssor talks about / the **two** ways / **sea** creatures obtain nu**tri**tion / in the **deep** ocean. /

The **fir**st method / is an **ac**tive method. / As for the **fir**st example, / the pro**fe**ssor talks about /**ane**mones. / What I **lear**ned from the **lec**ture is / that **ane**mones use their **poi**sonous **ten**tacles to catch pr**ey**. The **ten**tacles pa**ra**lyze the prey, / and **ane**mones ab**sor**b the nu**tri**tion / out of the **cau**ght fish.

The **se**cond method / is a **pa**ssive method. / As for the **se**cond example, / the pro**fe**ssor talks about / **oy**sters. / What **she** mentioned in the lecture / is that **oy**sters live on the **ocean** bed / and let **ocean cu**rrents flow over their shells. / This is how **oy**sters get nu**tri**tion. /

해석 강의에서 교수는 심해에서 바다 생물들이 영양분을 얻는 두 가지 방법에 대해서 설명한다.

첫 번째는 능동적인 방법이다. 이에 대한 예시로, 교수는 말미잘에 대해 말한다. 내가 강의에서 배운 것은 말미잘이 먹이를 잡기 위해서 독이 있는 촉수를 사용한다는 것이다. 이 촉수들이 먹이를 마비시키면 말미잘은 잡은 물고기로부터 영양분을 흡수한다.

두 번째는 수동적인 방법이다. 이에 대한 예시로, 교수는 굴에 대해 말한다. 그녀는 강의에서, 굴은 해저에 살면서 해류가 껍데기를 지나가도록 한다고 말한다. 이것이 굴이 영양분을 얻는 방법이다.

Listening Script

Last class, we talked about the environment in the ocean bed and the conditions for living there. Today I would like to talk about fixed dwellers in the ocean bed. These fixed dwellers in the ocean bed live at the very bottom of the ocean floor. Since they are so far down, they are unable to receive nutrition from sunlight. As a result, they have developed their own ways of acquiring nutrition, which turn out to be surprisingly effective.

First of all, let's talk about the active ways anemones acquire nutrition. Anemones are quite famous for their poisonous tentacles. They use these tentacles to approach prey. When they

지난 시간에 우리는 해저 환경과 그곳에서 살기 위한 조건들에 대해 이야기했습니다. 오늘은 해저에서 서식하는 생물에 대해 이야기하려고 합니다. 해저 생물들은 대부분 심해저에서 서식합니다. 수심이 깊은 곳에서 살기 때문에 그들은 햇빛으로부터 영양분을 받지 못합니다. 따라서 그들은 영양분을 얻기 위해 그들만의 방법을 발전시켜왔는데, 이는 놀라울 만큼 효과적인 것으로 밝혀졌습니다.

첫 번째로, 말미잘이 영양분을 얻는 능동적인 방식을 살펴봅시다. 말미잘은 독성이 있는 촉수로 유명합니다. 먹잇감에게 다가가기 위해 이 촉수를 이용합니다. 말

wrap their tentacles around a small fish, the fish becomes paralyzed. This is when the anemones absorb nutrition from the fish. This is how anemones prey on fish. Since they actively acquire nutrition, they are able to hunt in the specific time that they feel deprived of nutrition.

The second method creatures deep down in the ocean use to obtain nutrition is a passive method. Many oysters stick on the ocean bed and live there. Since they do not move a lot, or almost not at all, they just allow the ocean current to flow on their shell. Then oysters filter out nutrients from the ocean water and obtain the nutrition that they need. Although this method may seem fairly passive, it is quite effective because the ocean current is consistently moving, providing a constant source of nutrition. There will never be a lack of nutrition unless the ocean water dries up.

미잘이 그들의 촉수로 작은 물고기를 둘러싸면, 그 물고기는 마비되기 시작합니다. 이때 말미잘은 물고기로부터 영양분을 흡수하죠. 이렇게 말미잘은 물고기를 사냥합니다. 능동적으로 영양분을 획득하기 때문에, 영양분이 모자라다고 느끼는 특정한 시간에 사냥을 할 수 있죠.

해저 생물들이 영양분을 얻기 위해 사용하는 두 번째 방법은 수동적인 방식입니다. 수많은 굴들은 해저에 달라 붙어 삽니다. 그것들은 많이 움직이지 않기 때문에, 어쩌면 전혀 움직이지 않기 때문에 껍질을 스쳐 흐르는 해류를 그냥 받아들이게 됩니다. 바닷물로부터 영양분을 걸러내고, 필요한 영양분을 얻는 것이죠. 이 방식이 너무나 수동적으로 보일 수도 있지만, 해류는 끊임없이 움직이면서 영양분의 공급원을 제공해주기 때문에 꽤 효과적인 방법입니다. 바닷물이 마르지 않는 이상, 영양분이 부족한 일은 없을 것입니다.

Task 1

> **Question** Summarize the points made in the lecture, being sure to explain how they cast doubt on specific points made in the reading passage.

서론

[리딩의 기본입장 및 반박문장] **While the author of the reading passage argues that** the artificial sweeter, sucralose is harmful to our health for three reasons, **the lecturer opposes the reading's assertion with counter views**.

본론 1

[강의 주장 및 부연 설명] **First of all, the speaker argues that** the research on rats eating artificial sugar and having shrunken organs is unrealistic. **This is because**, to lead to the same result, people have to consume a tremendous amount of sucralose, but people do not usually eat that much. [리딩 지문 반론] **This casts doubt on the reading passage's claim that** sucralose can damage the immune system, which is proven by the rat experiment.

본론 2

[강의 주장 및 부연 설명] **Additionally, the lecturer points out that** the poisonous and dangerous molecule of sucralose that the reading mentions is not absorbed in our body. **Therefore**, it is not detrimental but very safe. [리딩 지문 반론] **This refutes the reading passage's assertion that** sucralose is toxic chemical, so its subsequences are unpredictable and dangerous in the long run.

결론

[강의 주장 및 부연 설명] **Finally, the professor contends that**, sucralose can be used when making sweet desserts. **What is more**, since people will consume less sugar with the use of the artificial sweetener, they will be healthier. [리딩 지문 반론] **This contradicts the idea presented in the reading passage that** the sugar substitute is unlikely to solve obesity problems, and rather it causes people to eat more sweet foods. [213 단어]

서론

독해 지문의 저자는 인공 감미료인 수크랄로스가 세 가지 이유들로 인해 우리 건강에 해롭다고 주장하는 반면에, 강사는 반대 의견들로 독해 지문의 주장을 논박한다.

본론 1

우선, 화자는 쥐들이 인공 설탕을 먹고 장기가 수축되는 연구가 비현실적이라고 논증한다. 이는 같은 결과로 이어지기 위해서는 엄청난 양의 수크랄로스를 먹어야 하는데, 사람들은 보통 수크랄로스를 그렇게 많이 먹지 않기 때문이다. 이것은 수크랄로스가 면역 체계를 손상시킬 수 있고 이것이 쥐 실험에서 입증되었다고 말하는 독해 지문의 요지에 의심을 불러일으킨다.

본론 2

게다가, 강사는 독해 지문에서 언급하는 수크랄로스의 유독하고 위험한 분자가 우리 신체에는 흡수되지 않는다고 지적한다. 그러므로, 이 분자는 해롭지 않고 안전하다. 이것은 수크랄로스가 독성 화학물질이기 때문에 앞으로 일어날 결과를 예측할 수 없다는 독해 지문의 주장을 반박한다.

결론

마지막으로 교수는 달콤한 디저트들을 만들 때 수크랄로스가 사용될 수 있다고 주장한다. 더욱이 인공 감미료를 사용하면서 사람들이 보다 적은 설탕을 소비할 것이기 때문에 사람들은 더 건강해질 것이다. 이는 설탕 대체물이 비만 문제들을 해결할 것 같지 않으며, 오히려 사람들이 단 음식들을 더 많이 먹게 될 것이라고 독해 지문에 제시된 의견을 반박한다.

Reading Passage	Sucralose

Sucralose - harmful

Recently sugar has been attacked by many health experts who claim that it is unhealthy and causes **obesity**. However, most foods in **industrialized nations** today contain large amounts of sugar as consumers prefer the sweet taste. Therefore, there have been recent attempts to create a substance both sweet and healthy. Sucralose is an artificial sweetener created for this; however it has many negative side effects.

수크랄로스 – 해롭다

최근에 설탕은 건강에 해롭고 비만을 유발한다고 주장하는 많은 건강 전문가들에 의해 공격받아왔다. 그러나 소비자들이 단맛을 선호하기 때문에 오늘날 산업화된 국가들의 대부분의 음식들은 많은 양의 설탕을 함유하고 있다. 그러므로, 달고 건강에도 좋은 물질을 만들기 위한 최근의 시도들이 있어 왔다. 수크랄로스는 이것(달고 건강에도 좋은)을 위해 만들어진 인공 감미료이다; 하지만 수크랄로스는 많은 부정적 측면을 갖고 있다.

<table>
<tr><td>

1. Damaging immune system
- Rats (experiment)

This sucralose has been shown to be damaging to the immune system. An experiment with rats shows that this artificial sugar can cause certain organs to shrink. As these organs **shrink**, the immune system is also weakened. The body becomes more **susceptible** to many different kinds of diseases. Large amounts of damage to the immune system can lead to disease and death.

</td><td>

1. 면역 체계 파괴
– 쥐 실험

수크랄로스는 면역 체계에 손상을 입히는 것으로 드러났다. 쥐들을 이용한 실험은 이러한 인공 설탕이 특정 장기들을 수축시키는 원인이 될 수 있다는 것을 보여준다. 이러한 장기들이 수축하면, 면역 체계 또한 민감해진다. 신체는 많은 다양한 종류의 질병들에 약해지게된다. 면역 체계의 많은 손상은 질병과 죽음으로 이어질 수 있다.

</td></tr>
<tr><td>

2. Containing a toxic molecule

The reason for such damage may be because of the way scientists created this sucralose substance. Sucralose is made by replacing a **molecule** found in regular sugar with a chemical compound that is poisonous and toxic to most animals and plant life. Although some say that this molecule is harmless, no one knows how this toxic molecule may affect humans in the long run.

</td><td>

2. 독성의 분자 포함

이러한 손상의 이유는 과학자들이 수크랄로스 물질을 만드는 방법 때문일지도 모른다. 수크랄로스는 일반 설탕에서 발견되는 분자를 대부분의 동물들과 식물들에 해롭고 유독한 화학적 화합물로 대체함으로써 만들어진다. 몇몇 사람들이 이 분자가 무해하다고 말함에도 불구하고 장기적으로 이 독성 분자가 사람에게 어떻게 영향을 미칠지는 아무도 모른다.

</td></tr>
<tr><td>

3. X solve obesity problems
- ppl want more sweet foods

Also, this substitute will not solve obesity issues in the end, because people will want more sweet food. As the body naturally **craves** sugar, there will be natural **cravings** for people to find foods that have sugar in it. However, since sucralose is not sugar, people will end up eating more sweet foods in an attempt to try and appease the sugar craving. This will lead to obesity.

</td><td>

3. 비만 문제 해결이 불가
– 사람들이 단 음식을 더 많이 원함

또한 사람들이 단 음식을 더 많이 원할 것이기 때문에, 이 대체물(수크랄로스)은 결국 비만 문제를 해결하지 못할 것이다. 우리 몸이 자연스럽게 설탕을 갈망하기 때문에 사람들이 설탕을 함유하고 있는 음식을 찾는 자연적 갈망들이 있을 것이다. 그러나, 수크랄로스는 설탕이 아니기 때문에 사람들은 설탕의 갈망을 달래기 위해 결국은 단 음식들을 더 많이 먹게 될 것이다. 이는 비만을 초래할 이어질 것이다.

</td></tr>
</table>

> **어휘_** sucralose 수크랄로스(단맛을 내는 인공 감미료) obesity 비만 industrialized nations 선진 산업국 side effects 부작용 shrink 줄어들다, 오그라들다 susceptible 민감한 molecule 분자 crave 갈망하다

Reading - flawed

Hello class. Today's topic is on sucralose, an artificial sweetener. You guys probably all regulary hear in the news about how obesity is a problem in our country, right? Well, in response to this, sucralose was developed so that we can keep eating sweet things without the negative weight impact. The article gives some arguments for why sucralose is bad, but I think the reasons that the reading gives are pretty weak. Here is why.

리딩은 문제 있음

여러분 안녕하세요. 오늘의 주제는 인공 감미료인 수크랄로스입니다. 아마 여러분 모두 우리나라에서 비만이 얼마나 문제인지 뉴스에서 자주 들을 거예요. 그렇죠? 수크랄로스가 개발되었기 때문에(개발됨에 응답해서) 부정적인 충격없이 우리는 단것들을 계속 먹을 수 있어요. 기사는 왜 수크랄로스가 나쁜지에 대해 몇몇의 논거를 들지만, 저는 지문이 주는 이유들이 상당이 취약하다고 생각해요. 여기 이유들이 있습니다.

1. Unrealistic results of the experiment
- X applied to humans

Firstly, the experiment that the article refers to is a very flimsy argument. This is because if humans were to have the same reaction from eating sucralose as the rats did, humans would have to consume 4000 packs of it. There is simply no way that anybody is going to eat that much sucralose, so the results of this experiment are unrealistic to humans.

1. (쥐) 실험결과 – 비현실적
　 사람들에게 적용 불가

첫 번째로, 글이 언급하는 실험은 논거가 매우 약합니다. 왜냐하면, 만약 사람들이 수크랄로스 섭취에서 실험 쥐들이 보였던 반응들과 같은 반응을 얻으려면 4,000봉지의 수크랄로스를 먹어야 하기 때문입니다. 누구도 그렇게 많은 수크랄로스를 먹을 수는 없기 때문에 이 실험의 결과들은 인간들에게는 비현실적입니다.

2. The Molecule – safe
- X absorbed by humans
- X stored in fatty tissues

Also, the argument that there is a dangerous toxic molecule in sucralose that is not found in regular sugar is not true. You see, this form of molecule is unique and not easily absorbed by humans so it would not be stored in the fatty tissues. And since the toxin is not stored in the body, it cannot produce any bad effects. As far as I can tell, adding this molecule is perfectly safe for humans.

2. 그러한 분자는 안전함
– 인간들에게 흡수 안 됨
– 지방층에 저장 안 됨

또한, 일반 설탕에서는 발견되지 않는 위험한 독성 분자가 수크랄로스에 있다는 주장은 사실이 아닙니다. 여러분도 아시다시피, 이러한 형식의 분자는 독특하며 인간에 의해 쉽게 흡수되지 않으므로 지방 조직들 안에 저장되지 않을 것입니다. 그리고 독성이 신체에 저장되지 않기 때문에 어떠한 나쁜 영향도 주지 않습니다. 제가 말할 수 있는 것은, 이러한 분자의 첨가는 인간들에게 완전히 안전하다는 것입니다.

3. Used to make sweet food

- X dissolve under high Temp.

- ppl → healthier

Finally, the article says that people will still want to eat sweet foods even if there is an artificial sweetener because they crave sugar. However, sucralose can also be used to make sweet foods. For example, sucralose acts just like sugar and does not dissolve under high temperatures so it can be used when baking desserts. Thus people can be healthier by eating sweet foods without eating sugar.

3. 달콤한 음식을 만드는 데 사용 가능

– 높은 온도에서 분해 안 됨

– 사람들이 더 건강해질 수 있음

마지막으로, 그 글은 아무리 인공 감미료가 있다고 하더라도 사람들은 설탕을 갈망하기 때문에 계속 단 음식들을 먹고 싶어 할 것이라고 말합니다. 그러나, 수크랄로스는 단 음식을 만드는 데에도 사용될 수 있습니다. 예를 들어, 수크랄로스는 일반 설탕처럼 작용하며 고온에서 용해되지 않기 때문에 디저트들을 구울 때에도 사용될 수 있습니다. 따라서 사람들은 설탕을 먹지 않고도 단 음식들을 먹으며 보다 건강해질 수 있습니다.

어휘_ a pack of ~ 한 봉지 unrealistic 비현실적인 a fatty tissue 지방조직 an artificial sweetener 인공 감미료 dissolve 용해되다 bake (빵 따위를) 굽다 a dessert 디저트

Task 2

Question Do you agree or disagree with the following statement?

It is important for the government to provide money to things that are beautiful and not just for things that are practical.

Use specific reasons and details to support your opinion.

서론

[GS] **Some people take it for granted that** the government should spend budget just on empirical things to boost the economy. [Thesis] **However, contrary to this idea, I strongly believe that** the governments should finance beautiful things. [Rationale] **The compelling logic behind this is that** this helps people to relieve stress and improves the economic situation of a society.

[GS(General Statement)] 도입 [Thesis] 자신의 입장 [Rationale] 근거, 소개

본론 1

[TS] **To begin with**, aesthetic objects allow people to alleviate their stress. [SS] **This is mainly because** unlike investment in practical things, investing in appreciating beautiful things ranging from artifacts in the national museum to national parks with spectacular natural landscape can help people relax and clear the mind. This enables a fresh approach to perplexing and stressful problems at school or work. Therefore, enjoying wonderful and good-looking scenery or artifacts is the easiest and quickest way to escape from the harsh reality that is full of piles of work and relationship problems. **[EG] For example**, I was extremely exhausted and stressed out due to many classes and homework when I was in college. One day, I visited a national museum that provided intriguing and beautiful artworks. As a result, I could have a brief moment of relief from my stressful work by appreciating the beauty of art and taking pictures. If I had not visited the national museum, I would have undergone a time of depression and despair.

[TS(Topic Sentence)] 소주제문 [SS(Supporting Sentence)] 뒷받침 설명 [EG(Example)] 예시

본론 2

[TS] In addition, the governmental investment in beautiful things encourages the growth of the economy. **[SS] An important reason is that** beautiful places that the government financially aids such as a national park with spectacular landscape and art works can attract tens of thousands of people to a community. As a result, local businesses such as restaurants, snack shops, and souvenir stores became to have more and more customers. On top of that, a number of jobs related to the stores were created. **[EG] From my experience**, the town I lived suffered from the economic recession. Fortunately, the government noticed that my town has some beautiful sites and started financing the beautiful spots in order to develop them as a national park. The advent of national park in my town revitalized the local economy by providing numerous employment opportunities ranging from ticket sellers to parking attendants and bringing more profits to stores in the society. In addition, several investors bought buildings and started family restaurants and shopping centers because the town became economically promising.

결론

[Restatement] In conclusion, without any hesitation, I firmly believe that it is essential for government to finance beautiful things as well as practical things. **[Summary] The reason is that** this helps people relieve their stress and facilitates the economic growth. [444 단어]

[Restatement] 재주장 [Summary] 이유 요약

당신은 다음 글에 동의하는가, 아니면 반대하는가?

정부가 실용적인 것들에 투자하는 것보다 아름다운 것들에 투자하는 것이 더 중요하다.

구체적인 이유와 상세한 설명을 통해 자신의 주장을 설명하시오.

찬성

❶ 스트레스 해소: 아름다운 풍경들과 예술작품들을 감상

❷ 경제 발전: 아름다운 것에 대한 투자가 관광산업을 발전시킴

서론

[GS] 몇몇 사람들은 정부가 경제를 부양하기 위해서 예산을 당연히 실용적인 것들에 사용해야 한다고 여긴다. [Thesis] 그러나 이러한 생각과는 반대로 나는 정부가 아름다운 것들에 돈을 써야 한다고 강력히 믿는다(아름다운 것들에 투자해야 한다고 강력히 믿는다). [Rationale] 이를 뒷받침하기 위한 설득력 있는 근거로는 아름다운 것들에 돈을 투자하는 것이 사람들에게 스트레스를 해소하게 하고 사회의 경제적 상황을 개선시킨다는 것이다.

본론 1

[TS] 우선, 미학적인 물건들은 사람들의 스트레스를 완화시켜준다. [SS] 실질적인 것들에 투자하는 것과는 달리, 국립박물관의 인공물부터 장관의 자연 경치를 가진 국립공원들에 이르는 아름다운 것들을 감상할 수 있도록 투자하는 것은 사람들이 휴식하고 마음을 정화하게 도울 수 있다. 이는 직장이나 학교에서의 당혹스럽고 스트레스를 주는 문제들에 대한 신선한 접근을 가능하게 한다. 그러므로, 훌륭하고 보기 좋은 경치나 인공물들을 즐기는 것은 산더미처럼 쌓인 일과 관계 문제로 가득한 가혹한 현실에서 탈출하는 가장 쉽고 빠른 방법이다. [EG] 예를 들어 나는 대학생 때, 많은 수업들과 숙제들 때문에 극도로 스트레스 받았고 지쳤다. 어느 날, 나는 흥미로운 공예품을 전시하는 국립박물관에 방문했다. 그 결과 나는 예술의 미를 감상하고 사진들을 찍으며 스트레스 받는 일로부터 짧은 해소의 순간을 가질 수 있었다. 만약 내가 국립박물관에 가지 않았더라면, 우울하고 절망적인 시간을 경험했을 것이다.

본론 2

[TS] 게다가, 아름다운 것들에 대한 정부의 투자는 경제 성장을 장려한다. [SS] 중요한 이유는, 정부가 재정적으로 지원하는 멋진 경치의 국립공원 같은 아름다운 장소들과 예술 작품들은 수천 수만의 사람들을 지역 사회로 끌어들일 수 있기 때문이다. 그 결과, 레스토랑, 매점, 기념품 가게 같은 지역 사업체들은 더 많은 고객들을 유치하게 되었다. 무엇보다도, 그 가게들과 관련된 다수의 직업들이 생겨났다. [EG] 내 경험상으로, 내가 살던 도시는 경기 침체로 고통을 받았다. 다행스럽게도, 정부는 우리 도시에 몇몇 명소들이 있다는 것을 알게 되었고 그 명소들을 국립공원으로 개발시키기 위해 재정적 지원을 시작했다. 우리 도시에서 국립공원의 출현은 티켓 판매원들부터 주차 보조원들까지 다수의 고용 기회를 제공하고 지역 사회의 가게들에게 더 많은 이익을 안겨주며 지역 경제를 다시 활성화시켰다. 더욱이, 우리 도시가 경제적으로 유망해졌기 때문에 몇몇의 투자자들은 건물들을 샀고 패밀리 레스토랑과 쇼핑센터(사업)들을 시작했다.

Writing

정답 및 해설

결론

[Restatement] 결론적으로, 나는 아무런 망설임 없이 정부가 실용적인 것들과 마찬가지로 아름다운 것들에 돈을 쓰는 것(재정적으로 투자하는 것)이 필수적이라고 확고히 믿는다. [Summary] 그 이유는 아름다운 것에 투자하는 것이 사람들이 스트레스를 해소하도록 돕고 경제 성장을 촉진하기 때문이다.

결론

[Restatement] 결론적으로, 나는 아무런 망설임 없이 정부가 실용적인 것들과 마찬가지로 아름다운 것들에 돈을 쓰는 것(재정적으로 투자하는 것)이 필수적이라고 확고히 믿는다. [Summary] 그 이유는 아름다운 것에 투자하는 것이 사람들이 스트레스를 해소하도록 돕고 경제 성장을 촉진하기 때문이다.